T0142460

THE STATUS OF
WOMEN
IN THE MUSLIM WORLD

SHAMIM ALEEM

authorHOUSE

AuthorHouse™
1663 Liberty Drive
Bloomington, IN 47403
www.authorhouse.com
Phone: 833-262-8899

Published by AuthorHouse   02/19/2021

ISBN: 978-1-6655-1592-4 (sc)
ISBN: 978-1-6655-1593-1 (e)

Contents

PART III

Preface

ON THE WORLD MAP MUSLIM countries occupy a very prominent place. There are more than fifty countries having a very high percentage of Muslim population (ranging between 100 to 90%) then there are over thirty countries where Muslims are in minority. Muslim countries are spread over every nook and corner of the world, they have a very diversified and interesting background.

Islam is comparatively a new religion, (7th century) it took birth from Arab countries and gradually spread over in different parts of the world. These countries already had their civilization, culture and traditions, when Islam became their dominant religion, it mingled up with their culture and traditions. Maldives, which has 100% Muslims population was dominated by Buddhism for 1400 years before it was converted into Islam in 12th century. Indonesia had 300 distinctive ethnic and religious group with 700 languages, when by the end of 16th century, Islam supplanted Hinduism and Buddhism. Azerbaijan was a part of Soviet Union until it got independence in 1991. Tunisia was a part of Ottoman Empire and had highly diverse culture. Nigeria which was earlier under the British rule, had 250 ethnic groups and more than 500 languages.

Today when we look at the Muslim countries, we find great difference in their civilization, culture and traditions, in spite of the fact that the foundation stone – the Quran and Sunnah - for all of them is the same.

The problem is that our imagination of a Muslim state goes by the stand point of the Quran and Sunnah but the reality is very different. Even those states, which have declared Islam as their state religion, have not structured their government and administrative machinery according to the provisions of the Quran and Sunnah. One reason for this lacuna is the struggle of political power in many Muslim countries, clubbed with the wrong interpretation of the Quran and Sunnah, defeating the very purpose of law.

In this background, to make an assessment of women's rights and status is not an easy job. Many states have a long list of laws guaranteeing equal rights to women. Practically all Muslim states are signatories to the international treaties that focus attention on women's rights especially on education, health, political and economic participation, and above all on violence against women. The signatory states are expected to follow the international guidelines but when we peep into the system the reality is different from the law books. The administrative mechanism of most of the countries is very slow, ineffective, corrupt and insensitive to women's problems. In most of the countries the attitude of the law enforcing agencies is very negative, which defeats the very purpose of law. In many other customs and traditions overruled the law. In practically all the countries, the patriarchal system dominates the scene and even if women are given rights, there is a demarcation (In Hindu mythology it is called Laxman Rekha) this far and no further.

In a recent survey (October 2018) conducted by the Bristol University on the social acceptance of domestic violence, people were asked if a husband or partner was justified in beating his wife or partner, if she goes out without telling him, argues with him, neglects the children, suspected of being unfaithful, refuses to have sex or burns the food. On an average 36% of the people thought it was justified in at least one of these situations. Surprisingly in 36 out of 49 countries (mainly in South East Asia and sub-Saharan Africa) women were more likely to justify the behavior than men.

The findings of the survey have made our job more difficult. In our struggle for gender equality our focus should be on attitudinal change - in all the people-especially among the male -who is the king of the decision-making process. But in this struggle if a woman suffers from inferiority complex and accepts her subordination, the battle is lost. What is needed is to make women aware of their rights and duties as laid down by the Quran and Sunnah and then pursue the government to implement them. It is not an easy job, the struggle for gender equality was going on for the past so many decades, but the success is slow, especially in Muslim countries. Now it is the responsibility of Muslim countries especially Organization of Islamic Cooperation (O.I.C) to take the lead and work out a model plan, in the light of the true spirit of the Quran and Sunnah and place it before the world.

The Quran has given an ideal plan of the relationship of husband and wife and the importance of family as the cornerstone of the society. Unfortunately, these issues have been diluted. I am still hopeful, the Quran has an answer for every human problem, we need to be honest and sincere in our efforts. I have made a modest attempt to look into the status of the Muslim women, the canvas is very wide, for detail analysis I picked up as a random sample of about a dozen Muslim countries, representing different regions and cultures. It is just the beginning, there is a long way to go. Please forgive me for my lapses. I look forward to your comments and suggestions.

As I was about to conclude my project on the Status of Women in Muslim world, there was a great blow to the rights and role of women all over the world due to COVID-19. I am scared that this pandemic may push back the progress of women made in many countries in the last few decades. I hope the women will face the new challenges with courage and determination.

Shamim Aleem
Austin, TX (USA).
Email: shamimaleem@hotmail.com

PART I

1

The Muslim World

TODAY ISLAM IS THE SECOND largest religion of the world, with a population of 1.57 billion representing over 23% of the world population. It is expected to be 9 billion by 2030[1]. The two primary branches of Islam are Sunni and Shia. The sects split from each other soon after the death of Prophet Mohammad (S) over a religious political leadership dispute about the rightful successor of Prophet Mohammad (S).

The great majority of Muslims, about 87 to 90% are Sunni. They regard the first four Caliphs as legitimate successors of the Prophet, and regard themselves as the original followers of Islam[4]. Followers of the Shia faith rejects the first three Sunni Caliphs and regard Hazrat Ali, the fourth Calipha as the true successor of the Prophet[2].

While Muslims are found on all the five continents, more than 60% of Muslim population is in Asia and about 20% in the Middle East and North Africa[6]. More than 300 million or one fifth of the Muslim population live in countries where Islam is not the majority religion such as India and China.
(*Muslim world Appendix 1*)

Shamim Aleem

Islamic Core Countries

Islam originated on the Arabian Peninsula in the first quarter of the 7th century. The faith has spread from there all over the world. The traditional heartlands of Islam are listed below.

State	Total Population	Capital	Notes
Saudi Arabia	34,218,000	Riyadh	Islam is the religion of the kingdom. Officially, all Saudi Arabian citizens are considered Muslims. Saudi Arabian citizens are 85-90% Sunni and 10-15% Shia (more than 30% of the country's population are expatriates or immigrants).
Yemen	29,826,000	Sana'a	An estimated 53% of the population is Sunni, and 45% is Shia. The Houthis, a Shia Islamic political and armed movement, have gained control of most of the northern part of Yemen's territory.
United Arab Emirates	9,890,000	Abu Dhabi	Islam is the official religion of the UAE. Just 20% of the population of the United Arab Emirates are UAE citizens. All Emiratis are Muslims; about 85% are Sunni, and 15% are Shia.
Oman	4,618,000	Muscat	56.4% of the population are Omani citizens, and almost all are Muslims (Ibadhi, the "third branch" of Islam, and some Sunni).
Kuwait	4,465,000	Kuwait (City)	The majority of Kuwaiti citizens are Muslim, with an estimated 60-70% Sunni and 30-40% Shia. The Kuwaiti population consists of 70% foreigners and 30% Kuwaiti.
Qatar	2,724,000	Doha	Islam is the state religion in Qatar. Qataris are all Muslims and followers of the Sunni Salafi version of Islam. Just 12% of the entire population are Qatari citizens.
Bahrain	1,503,000	Manama	Islam is the state religion in Bahrain. About half of the population are Shia, the other half Sunni.
Iran	84,000,000	Tehran	Shia Islam is the official state religion. Mashhad, Qom, and Shiraz in Iran are important Shia pilgrimage cities.
Iraq	40,223,000	Baghdad	Islam is the state religion in Iraq. The country is home to several important Islamic cities, such as Karbala, Najaf, Kazimayn (Baghdad), and Samarra.

Countries with the highest percentage of a Muslim population

A list of countries where the majority of the population is Muslim. There are about 30 countries where more than 90% of the citizens are followers of Islam.

1	Maldives	557,000	Malé	Islam is the state religion of the Maldives, and citizens are legally obliged to adhere to it. The Sharia, the traditional Islamic code of law, forms the basic legal code of the Maldives.
2	Mauritania	4,650,000	Nouakchott	Mauritania is an Islamic republic, and all Mauritanian citizens are (Maliki) Sunni Muslims.
3	Somalia	15,893,000	Mogadishu	Somalia is mainly an (Ash'ariyah) Sunni Islamic country and partly practices Sufism.
4	Tunisia	11,819,000	Tunis	In the constitution of Tunisia, Islam is declared the country's religion. About 99% of Tunisians are Sunni Muslims.
5	Afghanistan	38,900,000	Kabul	Virtually all people in Afghanistan are Muslims (99.7%), of which 80% - 90% are Sunni.
6	Iran	84,000,000	Tehran	Islam is the official religion in the Islamic Republic of Iran. 99.4% of the population are Muslims (Shia 90-95%, Sunni 5-10%).
7	Western Sahara	652,000	Tifariti	Large parts of Western Sahara are a non-self-governing territory; about 75% are under Moroccan control.
8	Yemen	29,826,000	Sanaa	Yemen's constitution declares that Islam is the state religion, and Arabic is the official language.
9	Algeria	43,900,000	Algiers	Islam is the state religion in Algeria. The vast majority of Algeria's citizens are Sunni Muslims.
10	Morocco	35,952,000	Rabat	An estimated 99% of the population adheres to Islam. About two-thirds of the Muslims in Morocco are Sunni Maliki.
11	Comoros	870,000	Moroni	The Comoros is the only predominantly Muslim country in southern Africa. About 99% of the population are followers of Sunni Islam.
12	Niger	24,207,000	Niamey	The vast majority of the population in Niger are practicing Muslims (99 %). Malikite Sunni, with Salafi influences, is the dominant denomination.
13	Saudi Arabia	34,218,000	Riyadh	Islam is the state religion in Saudi Arabia. The country is home to Mecca and Medina. The two holiest cities of Islam attract millions of Muslim Hajj pilgrims every year.
14	Tajikistan	9,314,000	Dushanbe	Tajikistan's population is 98% Muslim (about 95% Sunni and 3% Shia). The country is also home to some Sufi orders.
15	Palestine	5,101,000	Ramallah	Islam is the religion of the majority of the Palestinian Arab population in the State of Palestine (predominantly Sunni).
16	Jordan	10,756,000	Amman	The majority of the population of this religious and conservative country is Muslim (97.2 %, predominantly Sunni).
17	Djibouti	988,000	Djibouti	An estimated 98% of Djibouti's population are Muslims, with a Sunni majority (77%).
18	Libya	6,871,000	Tripoli	Most Libyans are Sunni Muslims. Islam, as practiced in North Africa, is often interwoven with the native Berber faith. [1]
19	Mayotte	280,000	Mamoudzou	Mayotte is a volcanic island group in the northern channel of Mozambique and part of the Comoros archipelago. The population of the French overseas territory is, as in the Comoros, predominantly Muslim.
20	Sudan	43,850,000	Khartoum	Sudanese Arabs make up the majority of the population, and (Sunni) Islam dominates life and politics in the country. Sudan has one of the largest Sufi communities in the world. [2]

21	Azerbaijan	10,067,000	Baku	Almost all Azerbaijanis are followers of Islam. Azerbaijan's Muslim population consists of about 85% Shiites and 15% Sunnis.
22	Pakistan	220,892,000	Islamabad	Islam is the state religion in Pakistan. More than three-quarters belong to Sunni Islam, while the rest is Shiite. Pakistan is home to the world's largest community of Ahmadi Muslims, an Islamic splinter sect.
23	Senegal	16,706,000	Dakar	96% of the Senegalese population are Muslims, and 95% of the faithful belong to a Sufi brotherhood.
24	Gambia	2,417,000	Banjul	95% of the population of the smallest country on the African mainland are Muslims. The majority of them follow Sunni laws and traditions.
25	Iraq	40,223,000	Baghdad	The population of Iraq is 75-80% Arab and 15-20% Kurdish. Islam is the state religion. The Muslim population is divided between Shiites (64-69%) and Sunnis (29-34%).
26	Kosovo	1,933,000	Pristina	About 93% of the population of Kosovo are Albanians. The majority of the inhabitants of Kosovo are Muslims (95%).
27	Mali	20,251,000	Bamako	Islam was introduced to West Africa in the 11th century. More than 90% of the population of Mali are (Sunni) Muslims.
28	Turkmenistan	6,000,000	Ashgabat	Turkmenistan's population consists of about 93% Muslims and 6% Eastern Orthodox, which are predominantly Russians.
29	Bangladesh	165,000,000	Dhaka	The state religion of the republic is Islam. 91% of the population of Bangladesh are Muslims, 8% are Hindus.
30	Egypt	101,097,000	Cairo	Islam is the dominant religion in Egypt. It is the state religion and is anchored in the Egyptian constitution of 2014.
31	Turkey	83,155,000	Ankara	Turkey's population is 70-75% Turks and about 20% Kurds. Islam is the dominant religion in Turkey; more than 99% are Muslims (mostly Sunni). Since 2003, the government under now President Erdogan is pursuing an explicit policy of Islamizing, not only of the educational system but the society as a whole. [3]

Countries with the largest Muslim population

List of countries with the largest Muslim population.

Country	Muslim Population	Muslim % of total Population	Notes
Indonesia	229,000,000	84%	Indonesia is the country with the highest number of Muslims. The overwhelming majority of Indonesia's Muslim population (99%) are Sunnis. Nevertheless, about one million adhere to Shia Islam (0.43%). Internal migration has increased the percentage of Muslims in formerly predominantly Christian eastern parts of the country.
Pakistan	202,650,000	92%	Islam in Pakistan emerged in the 7th century in Sindh communities along the Arab coastal trade routes. Today, Pakistan is the country with the second-largest Muslim population in the world.
India	195,000,000	14%	Islam is the second-largest religion in India after Hinduism. India has the largest Muslim population outside the majority of Islamic countries. India's Muslims are mainly Sunnis.
Bangladesh	153,700,000	93%	Most Bangladeshis are Bengali Muslims, a synthesis of Islamic and Bengali cultures.
Nigeria	109,254,000	53%	The country has the largest Muslim population in Africa. More than half of Nigeria's population is Muslim, predominantly Sunni. About 12% of Nigerian Muslims are Shiites. The main ethnic groups in Africa's most populous country are Hausa 30%, Yoruba 15%, Igbo (Ibo) 15%, and Fulani 6%.
Egypt	90,987,000	90%	Egypt is the most populous country in the Arab world. Islam is the state religion, according to the Egyptian constitution.
Iran	83,489,000	99.4%	All Iranians are Muslims, theoretically. The official state religion is Shia Islam. Iran is the country with the most Shiite followers. (90-95% Shiites and 5-10% Sunnis).
Turkey	80,660,000	97%	The predominant religion in Turkey is Islam (theoretically 97%). Turkey has been a fairly secular country since Atatürk, but in the last two decades, it has been largely ruled by Erdogan's AK Party, which is steeped in political Islam.
Algeria	43,460,000	99%	Algeria's population consists of 99% Arab Berbers. According to the Algerian Constitution of 2016, the state religion is Islam. 99% of Algerians are Sunnis.
Sudan	42,535,000	97%	Sudan's ethnic groups are Sudanese Arabs (about 70%), Fur, Beja, Nuba, and Fallata. Islam is the predominant religion in the country, and (Sunni) Muslims have dominated government institutions since Sudan's independence in 1956.
Afghanistan	38,783,000	99.7%	Islam is the official religion in Afghanistan. All Afghans are Muslim (99.7%: Sunni (Hanafi) 85-90%, Shia 10-15%).
Iraq	38,614,000	96%	Iraq's constitution states that "Islam is the official state religion". About 95-98% of the country's population is Muslim; (Shia 64-69%, Sunni 29-34%)
Ethiopia	38,283,000	33%	About one-third of the country's population are (Sunni) Muslims. The emigration to Abyssinia (Ethiopian Empire), also known as the first Hegira, was an episode in the early history of Islam when Muhammad's first followers (the Sahabah) fled Mecca from the persecution of the ruling Quraysh tribe.
Morocco	35,592,000	99%	Morocco is inhabited by mixed Arab-Berbers and Imazighen (Berber). According to Morocco's constitution, Islam is the state religion in the kingdom.

Uzbekistan	30,135,000	88%	The country's Muslim majority are (Hanafi) Sunni. Uzbekistan's government is opposed to a political Islam in the country. The Uzbek government eliminated the Islamic party in 1992, and one university had to close its Faculty of Islamic Studies.
China	25,000,000	1.8%	The Hui and the Uighurs from Xinjiang are the Chinese minority groups with the largest Muslim population. [4] China has blamed Islamic separatists from Xinjiang for a series of attacks on Han Chinese in recent years. Leaked government papers revealed China's crackdown on ethnic Muslim minorities in the Xinjiang region. [5]
Russia	25,000,000	17%	An estimated 17% of Russia's population are Muslims. [6] The Russian regions with the highest Muslim population are Ingushetia 96%, Chechnya 95%, Dagestan 83%, and Karachay-Cherkessia 64%.
Saudi Arabia	22,200,000	100%	Islam is the state religion. Saudi citizens are 85-90% Sunni and 10-15% Shia). Saudi Arabia is home to the two holiest cities of Islam, Mecca, and Medina where Islam originated.

Countries where Islam is the State Religion: -

26 predominantly Muslim countries have included Islam as the State religion, Afghanistan, Algeria, Bangladesh, Bahrain, Brunei, Comoros, Djibouti, Egypt, Iran, Iraq, Jordan, Kuwait, Libya, Maldives, Malaysia, Mauritia, Morocco, Oman, Pakistan, Palestine, Qatar, Saudi Arabia, Sahrawi, Republic, Somalia, Tunisia, United Arab Emirates, Yemen. The best example is of Libya, the most religiously diverse country in the Muslim world [3].

Albania	1,700,000	60%	Islam in the Balkans is an Ottoman heritage and is the largest religion in the Albania. About 60 % of Albanians consider themselves Muslims. The former communist country has closed mosques and churches in 1967. In November 1990, Albania allowed the private practice of religion again.
Bosnia and Herzegovina	1,673,000	51%	About half of the country's population are Muslims (51%); other denominations are Orthodox (31%) and Roman Catholic (15%).
Italy	1,600,000	2.6%	Italy has been for centuries a country on the front line where Islam and Christianity clash. Islam is not formally recognized by the Italian state. The country has an overwhelmingly Roman Catholic population (83%).
United States	3,450,000	1%	New estimates show U.S. Muslim population continues to grow. But only 1% of the total U.S. population are Muslims. [7]

List of European Countries with the largest Muslim Population.

Country	Muslim Population	Muslim % of total Population	Notes
France	6,000,000	9%	Islam is the second-largest religion in France. The country has the largest number of Muslims in the Western world, primarily due to migration from the Maghreb countries, West Africa, and the Middle East. Today about 9% of the population are Muslims.
Germany	5,000,000	6%	As a result of labor migration in the 1960s and 70s and several waves of political refugees since the 1970s, Islam has become the third largest religion in Germany after Roman Catholicism and Protestantism. About 6% of Germany's population are Muslims.
United Kingdom	3,373,000	5%	About 5% of the United Kingdom's population are Muslims, making Islam the second-largest religion in the country.
Russia	25,000,000	17%	Russia is a transcontinental country, 77% of Russia's area is in Asia. The regions in Europan Russia with the highest Muslim population are to the north of the Caucasus: Ingushetia (96%), Chechnya (95%), Dagestan (83%), and Karachay-Cherkessia (64%).

The Role of Shariah in Islamic Countries: -

In most of the Muslim countries, Shariah or Islamic law influences the legal code. Shariah means "Path" in Arabic. It provides guidance for all aspects of Muslim life. It is derived primarily from the Quran and the Sunnah. (The sayings, practices and teaching of the Prophet Mohammed(S)) Shariah developed several hundred years after the Prophet's death (632 CE)) collected by the scholars in the form of hadith. As each locality tried to reconcile local customs with Islam, the hadith literature grew and developed into distinct five schools of Islamic thought, they are: the Hanafi, Maliki, Shafiq, Hanbali, Shiite Jafari.

The five major schools of Shariah are broadly similar because they are derived from the same sacred sources. However, some schools take a more liberal approach to the text, while others allow for loose interpretations. And there are also important differences between Sunni and Shia Shariah. The Islamic Shariah is not an easily identifiable set of rules that can be mechanically applied, but a long and quite varied intellectual tradition [4].

These schools of thoughts have different impact on different regions of the Muslim world. The most orthodox school is Hanbali, which is mostly embraced in Saudi Arabia and Afghanistan. But since the last few years in Saudi Arabia there has been a liberal interpretation of Shariah, removing many restrictions on the way of women's progress, and gender equality. The Hanafi school which is supposed to be liberal is dominant among Sunnis in Central Asia, Egypt, Pakistan India, China, Turkey, the Balkans and Caucasus. North Africa is influenced by Maliki school and Indonesia, Malaysia, Brunei Darussalam and Yemen by Shafiq school. Shia Muslims follow Jafari school, most notably Shia dominated Iran.

Most Muslim countries continue to incorporate some traditional Shariah into their legal codes, especially in the area of personal-status law, which govern marriage, divorce and inheritance. In other areas of the law such as criminal code, most Islamic countries have attempted to limit the application of traditional Shariah, replacing it either with secular legislation or with laws characterized as modern interpretation of Shariah[5].

Many Muslim countries have a dual system, where the government is secular but the Muslims have the option to bring family and financial matters before the Shariah courts. The exact implementation differs from country to country but it is mostly practiced in countries like Nigeria, Kenya, Tanzania, Lebanon and Indonesia.

In many other countries like Saudi Arabia, Kuwait, Bahrain, Yemen and UAE where Islam is the official religion, Shariah is declared to be the source of law. In Pakistan, Iran and Iraq any legislation contrary to Islamic view is forbidden[6].

The secular Muslim countries, where the governments have declared to be secular in the constitution, like Azerbaijan, Tajikistan, Chad, Somalia and Senegal, are in minority. Popular Islamic groups are often viewed as a threat by existing governments and hence Shariah has a very limited role to play. Since 2011, in several Arab countries, like Libya, Tunisia and Egypt there was a wake of uprising, on the issue of Shariah law verses secular law, which ultimately busted many autocrats and helped Islamist political parties to come to power.

Today many debate on the question of compatibility of Islam with democracy. Many scholars say that there is no inherent discard between the two ideas, to support their view, they cite the examples of Turkey, Indonesia, Bangladesh, Mali and Senegal as democracies (Indonesia, is the world's largest Muslim nation.) Other countries such as Malaysia, Nigeria and Iran are nominally democratic as they lack many of the attributes of democracy. In the Arab world, countries like Syria, Libya, Tunisia and Saudi Arabia are the least democratic in nature. Other Arab nations fall somewhere between autocracy and democracy. The countries which are least democratic are Morocco, Algeria, Qatar and Yemen[7].

Among the Muslim countries some states like Afghanistan, Iran, Mauritanian and Pakistan have declared themselves as Islamic Republic (An Islamic Republic is a Sovereign state, that is officially ruled by Islamic laws and is not a Monarchy). Despite having similar names these countries differ greatly in their governments and laws. In 2010 the Organization of Islamic Cooperation (OIC), a group of 57 countries had only 5 democratic members: - Turkey, Malaysia, Indonesia, Bangladesh, Senegal and Pakistan. As of 2011, the list has included Tunisia, Egypt and Yemen[8].

More than a year after the first stirrings of the Arab spring, there continues to be a strong desire for democracy in Arab and other predominantly Muslim nations. Solid majorities in Lebanon, Turkey, Egypt, Tunisia and Jordan believe democracy is the best form of government.

While democratic rights and institutions are popular there is also a strong desire for the public life and Islam to have at least some influence on country's laws. Majorities in Pakistan, Jordan and Egypt believe that laws should strictly follow the teachings of the Quran, while most Tunisians and a 44% of plurality of Turks want law to be influenced by the values and principles of Islam, but not strictly follow the Quran[9].

References and Notes: -

1. Muslim Population (Master Doctorand - Muslim Population by Countries 2019
2. The Guardian - U.S edition October 2017
3. Pew Research Center, BBC Sunnis and Shia, the World atlas
4. Islamic Countries of the World: - World Atlas
5. Middle East: Islam and Democracy by Sharon Ottoman. 2005
6. Islamic Republic - Wikipedia
7. Islam: Governing under Shariah by Toni Johnson and Mohammad Aly Sergei. July 2014
8. The Middle East and Muslim Southeast Asia and Implications of the Arab Spring by Imtiaz Yusuf (Thailand)
9. Pew Research Center, Global Attitudes and Trends. 2012

2

The Status of Women in Islam

PEOPLE IN GENERAL HAVE A very biased view of women's status in Islam. They think that women are subjugated, degraded and oppressed, which is contrary to the basic principles of Islam and Sunnah. The Quran does not discriminate on the basis of sex, when it says

> "Men *and Women all descended from a single person: The Prophet Adam*[5]. *(the Quran 9.72).*

Men and women worship Allah in the same way. Allah judges all human beings fairly and equally.

> *"Allah has promised to the believers, men and women, gardens under which rivers flow, to dwell therein and beautiful mansions in gardens of everlasting bliss. (the Quran 9.72").*

These verses show that reward is dependent upon one's actions not gender. Islam took birth in Arabia in the seventh century. Culturally different parts of Arabia differed greatly from one another. There were some places such as Yemen that had reached the zenith of civilization. However, in general historians refer to this Islamic era of Arab as a period of Jahiliya (ignorance) or the age of darkness[1].

The social and moral values had degenerated to the lowest, for example there was no limit on the number of wives a man could have[2]. Burying a newborn girl was a common practice[3]. The women had no right to hold property, nor did they enjoy any other freedom. The establishment of Islamic state in Medina in 7 ADS by Prophet Mohammad (S) brought a new dimension to the status of women. For the first time they were treated equally. Prophet Mohammad (S) instituted rights of property, ownership, inheritance, education and divorce. Under Islamic laws, marriage was viewed as a contract in which the woman's consent was essential. The dowry, previously regarded as a bride price paid to the father, became a nuptial gift retained by the wife as a part of her personal property[4].

The historic records show that women prayed in mosques unsegregated from men. Women were encouraged to seek knowledge. Aisha (the Prophet's wife) had great authority in medicine and history[5]. Many women, converted to Islam prior to their husbands which shows women's right to independent decision-making. These rights improved the status of women and left the western women much behind in the race. According to professor William Montgomery Watt, "when seen in such historic context, Mohammad can be seen as a figure who testified on behalf of women's rights."[6]

Of course, no women held religious title in Islam, but many women held political power. There were many rulers in the pre-modern era, such as Khazana, who governed the Abbasid caliphs in the eighth century[7]. Malika Asma and Malika Arwa both held power in Yemen in the eleventh century.
(Influential Women in Islamic History. Appendix 11)

The Quran plays great emphasis on education and knowledge. The Quran begins with the word ***"Iqra"*** which means 'read'. Prophet Mohammad (S) said education is compulsory for every Muslim. He never differentiated between sexes. Aisha, the wife of the Prophet was the most scholarly person in the science of the Quran, poetry, fiqh, medicine, history of the Arab, and their geneology[8]. During his lifetime Prophet himself acknowledged Aisha's mastery over subjects. It is reported that he used to direct Muslims to make use of her education saying 'Take lessons from Humayra'[9]. Aisha used to conduct classes for women and children. The Prophet's another wife Hafsa bint e Umar Khattab was also very good at reading and writing. The Prophet had given special attention to her skills by appointing a teacher to help her. The Prophet also requested Shifa, who had an authority in the cure of insect bites, to teach this science to Hafsah.

Islam recognizes the individuality of women, where she is always known by her own name, not by the name of her husband, as practiced in the western society. If a woman is married more than once, every time she has to change her name tag which is a clear indication of subordination of women to men.

The Quran makes the concept of equality very clear, when it says that

> *"Men and Women are created from the same source." **(the Quran 4.1).***

When the essence of creation is the same, the argument of who is better and greater is redundant. A shift in the attitude of gender equality causes an imbalance in marital relationships leading to dysfunctional marriages. The Quran clearly mentions that husband and wife have equal rights over each other,

> *"And for women are rights over men, similar to those of men over women."* (the Quran 2.228)

The Quran has again emphasized the relations between husband and wife when it mentions;

> *"And among his signs is that He created your wives among yourselves that you may dwell in tranquility with them and He has put love and mercy in your hearts."* (the Quran 30.2).

Love, affection, understanding and sacrifice are the basic principles for a happy married life. The Prophet has repeatedly emphasized that;

> "the best of you are those who are best in treatment with their wives".

The Quran in one sentence has beautifully described the relationship between husband and wife;

> "They are clothing for you and you are clothing for them." (the Quran 67.14).

Clothing provides comfort, warmth and security as well as making one look good. Clothes protect you from the severity of weather and provide comfort to you. When you wear good clothes you not only look good but you also feel happy. Hence the relationship between husband and wife should be like good clothing helping and supporting each other and making them happy. But many people do not understand this message. Some of them think women are like clothes, you can change them whenever you want and throw them away when you don't need them.

Another issue which needs attention is polygamy (the practice of taking multiple wives). Many time Islam is attacked by its critics on this issue. Here is also a misunderstanding as the critics have not read in between the lines. In the pre-Islamic society of Arab, polygamy was the order of the day. In fact, a person used to have ten to twelve wives. it was in this background that the Quran says;

> "Marry women of your choice, two or three or four, but if you fear that you shall not be able to deal justly (with them), then (marry) only one, that it will be more suitable to prevent you from doing injustice." (the Quran AN Nysa 4.3)

Viewed in the proper context, it is clear that the Quran did not give a free license for having up to four wives, rather it was a restriction on the prevailing practice to cut down the maximum number to four. A close examination reveals that the wordings of surah, leaned towards monogamy[10].

The same message is given by the Committee on the Elimination or Discrimination Against Women which recommended that polygamy marriage should be discouraged and prohibited because its inherent disregards to women's right to equality with men[11].

Violence Against Women: -

There is no place in the Quran for violence against women. The Quran repeatedly has emphasized the way a wife should be treated. Only in one place the Quran has given the right to the husband to beat his wife.

> *"As to those women on whose part you see ill conduct, admonish them first, next refuse to share their beds, last beat them (lightly, if it is useful) but if they return to obedience, seek not against them means (of annoyance)." (the Quran 4.34)*

In the above verse Allah refers to the case of a wife who behaves immorally towards her husband's right. Even though it is such a sensitive issue, Allah advised the husband to be patient and follow the steps one by one. If all other steps fail, he is allowed to beat his wife, but here he is warned not to hurt her, not to break her bone, not to leave black and blue marks on the body, and avoid hitting her on the face or especially on sensitive places at any cost.

Many scholars and commentators have emphasized that hitting even where permitted is not to be harsh. According to Abdullah Yousuf Ali and Ibn Khatri, the consonance of Islamic scholars is that the above verse describes a lighting beat. The surah has to be understood in the proper context and if practiced in the right way, there is no scope of domestic violence in Islam. The pity is that critics just pick up some words without understanding the correct message.

The Prophet Mohammad (S) had eleven wives, the two died in his lifetime, the nine wives were with him till his death. But he never beat any of his wives though some of them were very out-spoken and used to pick up arguments with him. Leave aside the question of beating, he never even raised his voice or abused them. Once the Prophet was not happy with the behavior of his wives. He simply retired to the upper portion of the house, which was generally used as an area for storage. He never contacted his wives for a month (Illa) But he never abused them.

Gender equality is a relatively new concept in western democracy, various forms of discrimination (which of course still exist) were common and tolerated until a few decades ago. Many of the problems faced by Muslim women for example, domestic violence, or husband's refusal to allow his wife to work, are not problems unique to Islam by any means. They persist all over the world. One can argue that a cultural milieu exists in many Muslim countries that subordinate women. It will not be out of place to paint a picture of violence against woman, especially domestic violence in the international scenario. The United Nations along with its numerous agencies such as UNESCO, ILO, UNICEF, UN, Human Settlement have been trying hard to reduce domestic violence. A number of international agreements have been prepared and signed by a large number of countries to eliminate violence against women. Many countries have introduced new legislation to control domestic violence but in spite of all these efforts, domestic violence still persists, both in developed and developing countries. The U.N report on the progress of the World's Women 2019-2020 mentions "Within Family women and girls too often face violence and discrimination over their lifetime, around one in three women can expect to experience physical violence or sexual abuse at the hands of an intimate partner. In the U.S approximately 1.3 million women are being physically assaulted by an intimate partner annually [12]. In Russia, one in four families experience domestic violence. In the light of the above facts, it is not at all justified to blame Islam for domestic violence [13]. Domestic violence is inherent in the system from the beginning, which is a reflection of the patriarchal theory. No amount of legislation will stop domestic violence, what is needed is proper education and endurance to bring an attitudinal change, which is the only lasting solution.

A detailed examination of the provisions of the Quran and the life of the Prophet, clearly shows the high status of women in Islam. A woman can perform all the functions within the limits laid down by the Quran. The happiness of the family and the society at large, depends on the way these laws are implemented. The tragedy is that these laws have been diluted with the local customs and traditions where patriarchy has a great influence. It is easy to change the rights of women in the law books, but nothing will bring a drastic change unless there is a change in the mind set.

References and Notes: -

1. Aleem, Shamim: Women, Peace and Security - An International Perspective. 2013
2. Ibid
3. Aleem Shamim: Prophet Mohammad(S) and his family. A Sociological Perspective. 2011
4. Ibid
5. Ibid
6. Women in Islam. Oxford Islamic Studies.
7. Aleem Shamim: Prophet Mohammad (S). opp. cited
8. Ibid
9. Ibid
10. Progress of the World's Women 2019-2020- Families in the Changing World.
11. Ibid
12. Full report on the Prevalence Incidence and Consequences of Violence. Against Women National Institute of Justice 2013.
13. Violence Against Women on the Russian Federation ANNA

3

The Significance of Marriage and Family in Islam

ISLAM PLACES GREAT IMPORTANCE ON the institution of marriage as from here the family flourishes. The Quran explains;

> *"Allah has made for you, your mates of your own nature and made for you out of them, sons and daughters and grand-children and provided for you sustenance of the best." (the Quran 16.72).*

It clearly shows that there is no monasticism in Islam. The Prophet Mohammed (S)had advised the young men to marry, when he said;

> **"O young men, whoever is able to marry, should marry, for that will help him to lower his gaze and guard his modesty."** (Al-*Bukhari*).

The Prophet further says **"marriage is my sunnah, whosoever keeps away from it, is not from me."** (Al-*Bukhari*).

Islam does not approve pre-marital sex relations, nor does it believe in living together. Rape is considered a very serious crime.

The only way for biological needs of human beings is through the institution of marriage. In contrast to this, in many societies there is no restriction on pre-marital sex or living together, which results in single mothers and broken families, which in turn generates social tension. The main object of marriage according to the Quran is to enable human beings to dwell in peace and tranquility. In order to have peace, certain conditions must be met. These pre-request to peace are justice, fairness, equity, equality and fulfillment of mutual rights. Therefore, any injustice cannot be tolerated if the peace is to be maintained in the home. In the domestic sphere, oppression is manifested when one partner (in most cases the husband) makes unilateral decisions and applies a dictatorial style of leadership. Peace is compromised. Persecution is present when there is any form of domestic abuse being perpetrated. The Quran is very clear on the question of relationship to be maintained in the family. There is no scope for dictatorial behavior of the husband, even though he has the financial responsibility of the family.

Another principle on which family life is based in Islam is Rahimah (mercy). Allah says that he has placed mercy between the hearts of spouses. The mercy is manifested through compassion, forgiveness, care and humility. Allah further says that He has placed love between spouses. The love not in the sense in which it is manifested in the present society. Love is actually a sacrifice. When husbands and wives sacrifice their desire, time, and wealth for the sake of each other, that is the real love. Real happiness in the family is found when there is an element of sacrifice. This sacrifice gives a lasting bond of love and peace.

A deep insight into the family life of the Prophet Mohammad(S) shows that his family life was based on principles, laid down in the Quran. In his married life of 38 years there was not a single complaint by any wife against his behavior as a husband. On the contrary there were many instances where his wives could be blamed. Though he occupied such a high position in society but at home he always behaved like an ordinary person. Even though he has a busy schedule, not only he used to do his own work but was always prepared to give a helping hand to his wives, in the household work.

It is very disheartening to know that Muslims did not follow the Sunnah and the family gradually lost its significance. A narrow interpretation of Quranic laws clubbed with the local customs and traditions started deteriorating the status of women. In the last few decades in western society the emphasis has shifted from family to individual, from "'our" to 'mine'. The individual became the focus of attention. The basic norms of the family were diluted. The moment a child becomes an adult he thinks, he is independent, breaking his relationship with family. This resulted in making the very foundation (family) weak and creating social tension, destroying the peace of the family and the world at large. The international community has taken note of this new trend and has focused attention on the significant role of family in the society. The U.N. Women in its report on Progress of the Women 2019-2020 - 'Family in a changing world', has rightly mentioned that 'No institution has more universal and personal significance to each of us, than the family'. Families are places of love and nurturing where we can go for support and nourishment, especially in the times of hardship where we may bear and raise children and care for those in need.'

At the heart of this report is a recognition of the vital importance of families to our culture and economies. The report in its Executive summary has rightly pointed out that 'Families are a building block of societies without which communities and economies could not function.........' The report endorses the views of the Quran when it mentions that "Family into a home for equality and justifies a place where women can exercise voice and agency and where they have economic security and physical safety."

The report is also aware of the fact that this ideal picture of the family is not the truth of the day. Families can be 'make or break for women'. It elaborates the fact that within families, women and girls too often face violence and discrimination over their lifetime, around one in three women can expect to experience physical or sexual abuse at the hands of an intimate partner. The report further explains the reason for this abuse of power. It says that family is an institution that has historically been a stronghold of patriarchy and embodied men's social power-domination over women. It has been inscribed in laws and social norms across large and social swathes of the world during the periods of state-building and western colonization.

The above statement makes it very clear that there is no relation between the domestic violence and the Islam. It is an ongoing thing from the very beginning. In fact, the Quran painted a very rosy picture of the family, which would have brought peace and happiness in the world, if it would have been implemented in the right direction.

4

The Importance of Motherhood and The Dual Role of Women

IN ISLAM THE FAMILY IS the basic unit on which depends the peace, prosperity and the happiness of the community and the world at large. But unfortunately, in the western society, the emphasis has been shifted from the family to individual. The individual became the focus of attention. The basic norms of the society have been diluted. In the present-day society family has gradually lost its place resulting in social tension in the society. Although the experience of family life is essentially universal, families themselves do not take one form.

In Islam, the mother who is the architect of the family enjoys great respect. Once a person asked the Prophet Mohammad(s) "Who among people is most deserving of my good treatment? "The Prophet said "Mother", then again he asked the same question the Prophet gave the same answer, the third time also when that person asked the same question, the Prophet gave the same answer "Mother". This indicates the high status attach to motherhood in Islam. But motherhood has great responsibilities attached to it. It does not end with giving birth to a child, but it actually begins, with the greatest responsibility that a mother has in shaping the personality of the child, for which she needs proper education and time. A mother who is not educated will not be able to produce an enlightened child. To take care of a child's health, nutrition, to help him in building his future, to cultivate right ethical and moral values, to be a good human being, mother herself needs proper education, time and vision.

Even if a mother is educated, she may not be able to fulfill her responsibilities if she does not have the time to spare, which is the case with most of the working women today. It becomes very difficult for a working woman to balance the dual role. In their zeal to compete with men, the interests of the family are sacrificed. Working women can no doubt provide more comforts to their children, but not the love and affection and attention which are essential nutrients for the development of a healthy child. Today most of the families in the western society suffer from the social crisis for which they blame the youngsters, but they do not look into the real cause of this crisis: lack of proper parenting. No doubt, women's involvement in the working force is essential, not just for making the nation's economy strong, but also for enhancing the status of women in society. But here comes the dilemma, on one hand we want women to go shoulder to shoulder to men in nation building, which means taking more responsibilities and giving more time to the jobs, and on the other hand, mothers are also expected to give time and attention to their kids. This conflict has to be understood in the proper context and needs remedial measures. Women with little kids (until they go to school) need more facilities like long term maternity leave, work from home facility, day care centers, safe and reliable transportation etc. But very few countries have focused attention on these problems. A survey, for example, of maternity leave in different countries of the world, shows great variation.
(Countries with the most liberal Maternity plan. Appendix 111 and Countries with less Maternity Plans Appendix 1v)

There are of course certain countries which are most liberal in maternity leave programs such as Sweden (480 days), Norway (400 days), and U.K (365 days), while there are countries with the least maternity leave like UAE (6 weeks), Switzerland (12 weeks), Germany (14 weeks) and Belgium (15 weeks). Most surprising is the case of the most advanced country of the world --- United States, - which does not guarantee maternity leave to mothers, it is left to the discretion of the employer. In many cases it is 12 weeks with or without pay, which is a subject of great concern.

Maternity leave across the Muslim world gives a gloomy picture. The most liberal among the Muslim countries is Morocco (14 weeks), Algeria (14 weeks), while many other countries give 12 weeks or less. Egypt (12 weeks), Kuwait (10 weeks) and UAE (6 weeks). it is disheartening to note, that none of the Muslim countries has a well-planned, progressive maternity leave plan. It is here that we see a lack of vision to fulfill the obligations for Motherhood as laid down in the Quran.

Of course, the Quran neither prohibits the mother from working nor mentions anything for a working mother. The emphasis on women joining the work force is comparatively of recent origin, to bridge the gender equality gap, and if the Muslim countries want women to join this new trend, then it becomes the responsibility of the government to create such an environment and provide such facilities where by mothers may be able to fulfil their commitment to the job and the family

It is true that most of the Muslim countries give a dark picture of women's rights. Women do not get the rights as laid down in the Quran and Sunnah. There are a number of unnecessary restrictions on the rights of women. Violence against women is a common phenomenon all over the world and Muslim countries are no exception to this. Today the world is facing the biggest challenge of gender equality. In the present context gender equality means that man and woman are equal. There is no difference and a woman can do any job, and hence there is always a competition between man and woman to reach to the highest ladder. The Quran does not accept this type of competition. It says;

> *"And the male is not like the female"* (*the Quran 67.14*).

The Quran gives equal rights to men and women in general but specific rights and responsibilities granted to them are not identical. Men and women have complimentary rights and responsibilities.

Apart from the physical differences, the scientists agree that there are many other subtle differences in the way the brains of men and women process language, information and emotion, just to mention a few. Edward O. Wilson of Harvard University, a socio-biology expert said that females tend to be higher than males in verbal skills, empathy and social skills among other things, while men tend to be higher in independence, dominance spatial and mathematical skills rank-related aggression and other characteristics.

Islam realizes this basic difference between the male and female and says that man and woman have complimentary, yet different roles best suited to their nature. In this age of specialization, for example, the two physicians who are equal in their positions, rank and salary perform different duties, depending on their specialization. The same theory should be applied to the role of man and woman in society.

A survey was conducted by Pew Research Center in 2012, in six Muslim countries (Lebanon, Turkey, Egypt, Tunisia, Jordan and Pakistan) to know their attitudes towards different issues. Majorities in all the six countries believe women should have equal rights as men. While many support the general principle of gender equality, there is less enthusiasm for gender parity in politics, economics and family life. For instance, many believe men make better political leaders, that men should have more of a right to a job than women when jobs are scarce. The opinion expressed in this survey reflects the Quranic principle that men and women are equal but not identical. The illogical foolish competition going on in the world today for the sake of gender equality has destroyed the peace of the family and the society at large. Women are crushed under the dual responsibilities of the job and the home. Children are suffering due to lack of time and attention from the mothers. Husband-wife relationships become tense because of lack of understanding and ego problems.

What is needed is the understanding of human nature and behavior. In any organization, the unity of command is an essential principle for the smooth running of the organization, which needs a clear demarcation of functions and responsibilities among the employees. The same principle needs to be applied in household management. In certain areas, women should have the freedom to use their discretion, while in others, men should have the final word. It is always desirable to have consensus on major issues. But for such a plan of action, man has to change his dictatorial attitude which is the outcome of the patriarchal system of society. The woman also needs to be properly educated to have a clear and broader vision of the things. Unfortunately, today the focus is on acquiring technical knowledge and degrees to help in getting a job, but no orientation is given on the issues of family life. The educational policies need to bring a drastic change and focus attention on the understanding of human nature. Today's mechanical society has made the human being a part of a machine denied feelings and emotions.

While for every job in the society there is a training or orientation course, but marriage and parenting are excluded from this list which is a big mistake. A well-planned orientation program for the parents should be made compulsory. In the interest of the happiness of the family and the society at large, there is a need to look at the things from a new perspective.

The Quran has provided the guidelines, if implemented in the right direction, a happy peaceful society can be established where everyone has to contribute his or her might to enjoy the fruits of eternal happiness. The Muslim countries should take a lead to prepare a well-designed programmed where by women can incorporate the rules of the Quran in their family lives, along with the present demands of the society.

PART II

1

The Republic of Azerbaijan

THE REPUBLIC OF AZERBAIJAN LIES in the borderlands of Asia and Europe. It is situated in the southeastern part of the southern Caucasus and shares borders with the Russian Federation, Islamic Republic of Iran, Turkey, Georgia, Armenia and Turkmenistan. Azerbaijan has an area of 86000 sq. km with a population of 9898100. It has a majority of Muslims (96.9%). But it is a secular state where religion is separated from politics. Christians constitute 3% and others 1% of the population. The Muslim population consists of Shiites (89%) and Sunni (10%)[1].

The Azerbaijan Democratic Republic proclaimed its independence in 1918 and became the first secular democratic Muslim state. In 1920 the country was incorporated into the Soviet Union as Azerbaijan. Soviet Socialist Republic of Azerbaijan proclaimed its independence on 30 August 1991. Azerbaijan is a unitary Semi-presidential republic. It is one of the six independent Turkic states and an active member of the Turkic council. It has diplomatic relations with 158 countries and holds membership in 38 International organization[2].

The constitution of Azerbaijan (25 November 1995) states that it is a presidential republic with three branches of power. The parliament is known as Milli Majlis, it is unicameral and consists of 125 elected members for a term of 5 years. The Executive power is held by the President, who is elected for a 7-year term by direct election. The President with the consent of Milli Majlis appoints the Prime Minister and other members of the Cabinet and can also dismiss them; they are accountable to him[3].

The country's leadership has remained in the Allayer family since Heydar Alien became president in 1993 and was succeeded by his own President Ilham in 2003 who was elected President for the fourth time in April 2018[4]. The government has significantly reduced the poverty rate and has directed revenues from oil and gas production to develop the country's infrastructure. However, corruption remains a problem and the government has been accused of authoritarianism[5].

The Status of Women: -

Universal suffrage was introduced in Azerbaijan in 1919. It is the first Muslim majority country to enfranchise women. The Constitution of Azerbaijan guarantees equal rights to men and women. To implement the law public authorities must regularly review legislation related to gender equality and amend it as necessary[6].

National legislation provides a strong legal foundation for gender equal access to economic resources. The Constitution and the laws guarantee women equal rights to own property and engage in all economic activities. The Constitution provides an adequate legal basis for the domestic implementation of International laws in general and International Human Rights Laws in particular. The International treaties to which Azerbaijan is a party are recognized as a Constitutional part of the integral legal system (Art.148) and give a higher hierarchical status in the case of a conflict with a national law. The Constitution empowers domestic courts to apply International Human Rights treaties to which Azerbaijan is a party. This is a very progressive assertion[7].

Political Rights of Women: -

Azerbaijan was the first Muslim majority country to grant universal franchise to both men and women in 1919. The women have the right to vote as well as to stand for election. The percentage of women in parliament is not very high, only 17% (2015)[8]. As of 2020 there were 22 women in the 125-seat parliament but women have occupied high posts in parliament such as Dy. Speaker of parliament, several Dy. Ministers. Women held the positions of Dy. Chairman of the constitutional court. Women were also the ambassador to different countries. There were 4 women (out of 16 members) in the Central Election Commission.

In 2017, Mehriban Aliyev (The President's wife) was appointed Vice President of Azerbaijan, the highest position a woman has occupied in Azerbaijan. Her active participation is not limited to philanthropy as a traditional form of social involvement for spouses of the head of the state. But it covers a wide range of responsibilities. She is a paragon of a public figure, a role model for women[9].

Civil and Personal Laws for Women: -

Though Azerbaijan is a Muslim majority state religion has practically no role to play in the lives of its citizens. Azerbaijan requires certification and registration for people performing religious rites. Muslim women can study to become certified mullahs and lead women-only gathering a unique local tradition that goes back centuries; as of 2016 there was one local female pastor in Azerbaijan[10].

Marriage is governed solely by Civil Law; and only marriages that have been registered at a state register office are legally recognized. Marriage performed in religious ceremonies has no legal standing. It is believed that more couples are marrying under Islamic law, especially in rural areas and not registering their marriages with the state[11]. Such marriages have no legal recognition and women's rights are poorly protected within them. According to the Family Code (November 2011) the minimum age for marriage both for men and women is fixed at 18 years. A child marriage is criminalized by the criminal code. But according to the information from various sources, it was found that there is an increase in the number of child marriage, in most of these cases girls are forced to marry against their will[12]. This practice is more common in rural parts of Southern Azerbaijan according to a survey conducted by the state statistics committee found that 63% of women who were married at an early age said they had been married against their will[13]. The U.N special Rapportage on Violence Against Women (2013) expressed concern about the increasing number of forced and unregistered marriages. As per the State Committee Report 5000 girls were victims of child marriage in 2013[14].

Family Code (Art. 56 to 61) gives to both parents the same rights and responsibilities in caring for and educating their children. Both have equal decision-making authority over children following divorce. Further the Family Code says that women and men can both be the head of the household. This clause seems to be a controversial one, especially in the case of disagreement between husband and wife. Though these laws are to be governed by civil code, the traditions and the practices are quite different.

The customary attitudes regarding gender roles within the household appear to be very strong. How laws are implemented in practice differ, men are seen as the head of the household and women are expected to obey them. As per the survey by the U.N Development Program (UNDA) (2007) it was found that in general men are considered the head of the family and this is accepted by both men and women[15]. By contrast, women are expected to seek an agreement from their husbands before making important decisions; which is a situation accepted by most women[16].

Women and men have the same rights to initiate divorce. It is noted that in cases where a marriage has not been registered with the state authorities' women have very little protection. They cannot claim joint ownership of any property purchased during the marriage. As per the Family Code women and men enjoy equal inheritance rights as wife and husband, and as son and daughter to inherit legally. Inheritance law is governed solely by Civil Law[17].

But in the customary practices, things are different in most communities. The youngest son in the family is expected to stay in the parental home and look after his parents. As a result, parents usually leave property to the youngest son meaning that daughters have little opportunity to inherit property. In addition, when a man dies, his authority as head of the family passes not to his wife but to the eldest son [18].

Economic Participation of Women: -

The Constitution provides equal opportunities to men and women in the economic participation of the workforce but there are social constraints specially from the family which restricts women's involvement in the labor force. Women are expected to fulfill their responsibilities as wives and mothers. The men generally do not prefer to share household responsibilities and hence women find it very difficult to balance their dual role [19]. Women have to be very cautious in choosing their jobs, taking into account the flexible working hours, distance from the house, maternity leave plans, facility of day care etc. Rural women prefer agriculture jobs as they are more comfortable in this field.

Although sex discrimination is illegal but the Labor Code of Azerbaijan prohibits women from joining 678 occupations which are considered unsafe for women such as mining, drilling, oil & gases [20]. Though Azerbaijan legislation ensures equal pay for the same job, in practice there is a high gender gap. Women earn 52% of what men earn. The country ranked 88 out of 135 (GGGI) [21]. Though there is no restriction on women joining civil services, the number of women is very low. They have a share of only 28.6%. Women have dominated in certain fields such as health and social work (77%), education (73%) [22]. As of 2017, 78.1% of all teaching staff (including 51.9% of all university lecturers) 64.9% of all medical staff and 40.2% of athletes in Azerbaijan have been women [23]. The women's unemployment rate is also high 59% (2017) as compared to men (41.1%) [24].

In spite of the fact that women in Azerbaijan have no legal restriction, they are equal before the law; the literacy rate is high (99.7%) as compared to men (99.9). Women continue facing gender-based restrictions and discrimination that are deeply rooted in patriarchal attitudes, traditional social norms and by strict gender roles and stereotypes. The male domination and gender are stronger in rural areas. Gender-specific barriers often accumulate and women have to struggle with an uncomfortable economic burden and patriarchal gender norms.

The findings of the study conducted in 2018 by Dr. Aysal Nazimova demonstrates that women require a much longer list of facilitating factors - family support, redistribution of domestic labor, greater mobility in public space and gender equal treatment by employees [25].

Education for Girls/Women: -

Azerbaijan is one of the Muslim majorities, secular state where religion is separated from politics and government has no role to play in the religious activities of its citizens. But in the Pre-Soviet period, Azerbaijan education included intensive Islamic religious training starting from early childhood when children attended madrasas (educational institutions affiliated with mosques). In 1865, the first technical high school and the first women's high school were opened in Bakell [26]. In the late 19th century, secular elementary schools were established. But the majority of ethnic children received no education in this period and Azerbaijan's literacy rate remained low especially among girls [27].

During the Soviet period, the Azerbaijan's educational system was based on the standard model imposed by Moscow which featured state control of all education institutes and heavy doses of Marxist-Leninist ideology at all levels [28]. Azerbaijan constitution provides free and compulsory primary and secondary education for all boys and girls. The first secular school for girls in the Muslims East opened in Baku in 1901; that has a special place. The appearance of the school consisted of the establishment of a new culture in Azerbaijan which combined elements of traditional Muslim and advanced European civilization. An important feature is the gradual transformation of views on the status of women's education and in general on the position of women in society[29]. The adult literacy is now almost universal 99.7% for men and 99.2% for women.

In the field of higher education, there were 38 state run and 11 private universities in 2016[30]. The gates of higher education are open to all men and women. In 2004, 28.79% of boys and 25.55% of girls took admission in the colleges[31]. Because of the role of the oil industry in the Azerbaijan economy a relatively high percentage of boys have obtained higher education in scientific and technical subjects. Girls' choice of subjects is limited due to various reasons. First of all, there is a ban on vocation where women cannot be employed due to a hazardous nature of job and hence this limits the scope of women in choosing technical subjects.

Secondly, in spite of the progress made in the field of education women are not free to choose their career as their basic responsibility is to look after the family and decision to take a job depends on the opinion of the family members. Women have to balance their dual role, and they prefer to take jobs in the traditional fields like education, medicine, and public health where they feel more comfortable.

Violence Against Women: -

The 21ST Article of the Republic of Azerbaijan guaranteed equal rights for men and women and aims to eliminate all forms of gender-based discrimination and ensure gender equality in the political, economic, social and cultural spheres. All human rights are guaranteed to women and men.

A law to prevent domestic violence was adopted on 22 June 2010. The law focuses on domestic violence between close relatives to mitigate its negative legal medical and social outcomes and provide legal and social assistance for victims. Although it does not state its aim is to protect women, women are the victims in most cases of domestic violence. The law accepts the prohibition of discrimination against women as a core principle.

Under the law, victims can apply to the court for short term and long-term protection orders which prevents the perpetrator from any contact with the victims. Non-compliance with a protection order can result in criminal prosecution.

The law includes a comprehensive mechanism to oversee the implementation of the law, laying out the responsibilities of the police, the courts and the other official bodies. However, the 2012 European Commission Neighborhood Policy Report on Azerbaijan noted that in fact, mechanisms are not in place for the effective implementation of the law[32]. Apart from the national legislation, Azerbaijan has been a party to many international treaties on violence against women. It has ratified the convention on the Elimination of all Forms of Discrimination Against Women in 1995. The first government report to the U.N Committee on the Elimination of Discrimination Against Women (CEDAW) was published in 1996.

With the help of the U.N Development Fund for Women (UNIFEM) Azerbaijan has taken up a project known as Women for Conflict Prevention and Peace Building. The aim of the project is to promote the activities of women's organizations and support activities, leaders and youth in gender activity, peace-building and conflict prevention. Rape is illegal and carries maximum punishment of 15 years prison sentence. But many people do not consider it a crime. An article published by the A Land Island Peace Institute states that prosecution in rape cases is rare, due to gender norms that stigmatize victims as well as high levels of corruption within the policeforce[33].

There is considerable social stigma attached to rape, very few women are willing to report. The ASP9 report says that women have often little faith that law enforcement bodies will offer protection and adequate assistance. Moreover, there are no trained personnel in the police department to deal with their cases.

Forced prostitution is another form of violence against women. Though it is an administrative offense rather than a crime and punishable by a fine of up to $102[34]. But most of the women working as prostitutes have been violently abused by their families. Some women have also taken this as a profession for money. In Shia community there is a provision of a Sighe marriage (marriage for a short period in exchange of money) which is like a prostitution.

Trafficking is a relatively new problem in Azerbaijan. Although it is difficult to obtain accurate statistics it is increasing though it would appear that Azerbaijan is currently favored more as a transit country by traffickers[35]. In Azerbaijan, cases of domestic violence are neither reported properly nor any systematic record is kept by authorities. In 2016, 110 women were murdered by husbands and close relatives. In 2017, 807 cases of domestic violence were reported[36]. Though the 2010 law includes a comprehensive mechanism to oversee the implementation of the law, it displays the responsibilities of police, the courts and other official bodies. However, the 2012 European Commission Neighborhood Policy Report on Azerbaijan noted that in fact mechanisms are not in place for the effective implementation of law[37].

According to a 2007 report by U.N. Development Program (UNDP) a large-scale survey on attitudes to gender issues in Azerbaijan found that society considers domestic violence to be a private matter and should be resolved within the family. A more recent article published by the ALand Island Peace Institute indicates that such attitudes are still prevalent[38].

Convention on the Elimination of All Forms of Discrimination Against Women (CEDAW) (2009) in its concluding Observations, expressed its concern that domestic violence and other forms of gender-based abuse appear at times to be socially legitimized by a culture of silence and impunity.

In the light of recent cases of often fatal violence against women and girls in Azerbaijan, the U.N urges immediate concerted action to protect women and girls at risk of all forms of violence and to hold accountable those responsible for committing such violence[39].

The ALand Island Peace Institute is very critical of the present situation of domestic violence. It has pointed out the gap between the technical legal situation and the actual situation of women in Azerbaijan as dramatic - few women are aware of their legally enforceable rights and cases of violence against women are rarely reported to the police. In Spite of the claim of Azerbaijan as a democratic country which respects and enforces human rights, it remains a very traditional post-soviet society where gender stereotypes prevail and social conventions regulate the behavior of men and women. In reality, decision-making is organized along patriarchal norms. Women are often deprived of the rights to independent decision-making, equal participation within the family, proper education and employment opportunities as compared to their male partner [40].

A survey was conducted in 2012 to get people's opinion about domestic violence in which 46% believed that women should tolerate domestic violence in order to keep their family together and 22% agreed that there are times when a woman deserves to be beaten [41].

Azerbaijan claims to be a democratic country, guarantees equal rights to men and women, respects human rights does not need new laws, it needs existing laws to be implemented strictly. It needs an awareness of the issue among all sections of the society, it needs a change in attitudes among men and women to ensure an understanding of violence against women as unacceptable.

References & Notes: -

1. A Guide to the Republic of Azerbaijan Law Research - GlobalX 6/8/2020 by Ramil Iskandar.
2. Azerbaijan: Membership of International groupings/organizations British Foreign and Commonwealth Office (2007)
3. Ibid
4. Ibid
5. Middle East: Azerbaijan. The World Factbook-Central
6. Law of the Republic of Azerbaijan on State Guarantees of Equal Rights for Women and Men.
7. Guide to the Republic of Azerbaijan Law Research. Opp. cited
8. Women in Azerbaijan. Wikipedia
9. Ibid
10. Ibid
11. According to the Food and Agriculture Organization (FAO) Gender and Land Rights Database - Social Institution and Gender Index-Azerbaijan.
12. Social Institutions and Gender Index - Azerbaijan. OECD Development Center.
13. Ibid
14. Ibid
15. Ibid
16. According to the Food and Agriculture Organization (FAO) Opp. Cited
17. Social Institutions and Gender Index - Azerbaijan. OECD Development Center. Opp. Cited
18. Ibid
19. Ibid
20. Ibid
21. UNDD Report. 2007
22. World Public Opinion Organization. 2009
23. Ibid
24. Social Institutions and Gender Index Opp. cited.
25. Ibid
26. Ibid
27. Ibid
28. Women in Azerbaijan - Wikipedia 2020.
29. Azerbaijan - Country Gender Assessment. December 2019

30. Women in Private Sector in Azerbaijan Opportunities and Challenges. Gender Assessment Report 2018 by Dr. AyselVazirova.
31. History of Education in Azerbaijan K12 academics. 6/13/2020.
32. Ibid
33. Ibid
34. First Secular School for Women in the Muslim East - IRS History by Farhad Jabbarow.
35. Higher Education in Azerbaijan K12 Academics.
36. Azerbaijan Gendcr Information Center National Status Report on Gender Education 2005.
37. OECD- Development Center-Social Institutions and Gender Index
38. Social Institute Opp. Cited
39. Statement by the U.N in Azerbaijan on Violence Against Women and girls - 21 October 2019
40. Gender based Violence in Azerbaijan. The ALand Island Peace Institute. 6/9/2020
41. Statement by the U.N in Azerbaijan on Violence Against Women and Girls - 21 October 2019.

2

Brunei Darussalam

BRUNEI IS AN INDEPENDENT ISLAMIC Sultanate on the northern coast of the island of Borneo in Southeast Asia. It is bounded to the north by the South China Sea and on all other sides by the East Malaysian state of Sarawak. It has an area of 5,765 km²; and a population of 428,963(2018). 82.70%population is Muslim. Brunei achieved independence in 1984, after having been a British protectorate since 1888 [1].

Brunei is composed of a mixture of Southeast Asian ethnic groups, nearly two-thirds of the population is Malaysian and one-fifth is Chinese and the remainder are Indo-Aryan people. But all groups get along to help maintain a safe, stable and secure country government by a monarchy that has been surviving for over 600 years. About two-thirds of the people it governs practice Islam but the government is tolerant of other religions and cultures also [2].

The Islam is the religion of the state. The official language is Malaysian with English as a major second language. Brunei's population is predominantly Sunni Muslim. In 1959 Brunei became a self-governing state and adopted a constitution; although the British retained jurisdiction over foreign policy, defense and internal security. In 1984, Brunei got full independence and an Islamic Sultanate was established while the constitution was retained with significant amendments.

The Sultan is both head of the state and government and the ultimate authority rests with him. As prime minister he presides over the Council of Ministers and is advised by several other councils (Religious, Privy, Succession and Legislative).

The constitution provides for the establishment of a Legislative Council known as Majlis Mesyuarat Negara. The members are appointed by the Sultan, and hold office during his pleasure.

Since the last 600 years the Sultan has been from the same family. The present Sultan is highly educated. He has specialized in many subjects and he has many important ministries under his supervision. He is a man of vision and has great appreciation for women's role in the national economy.

Brunei's economy is almost totally dependent on its vast reserves of petroleum and natural gas; which give the state a very high revenue. The per capita income of its citizens is one of the highest in Asia. But the government is also trying to diversify the economy by developing other sectors, such as agriculture, fisheries, tourism and financial services. Brunei at present has to rely on imports for nearly all its manufactured goods and most of its food.

Brunei is essentially a welfare state, education and healthcare are provided free of charge to every citizen, through a well-designed network of government centers scattered throughout the country even rural areas are also visited regularly by the government's flying doctor service. Due to its small size and limited population, the administration is able to cater to the needs of all its citizens. It takes care of even the housing and provides many facilities so that there are no homeless people. Though a monarchy but works like a welfare state, this has been made possible due to its limited population, abundance of wealth and an efficient administration machinery[3].

The Status of Women: -

Brunei's government believes that women's involvement in all aspects of the community is needed in the nation's development and that women carry with them a different perspective that provides balance in decision making. In a talk delivered at the

United Nations General Assembly in September 2015, His Majesty Sultan said that the pace of globalization lifelong learning has been given serious attention, he stated that girls and women have equal opportunities in upgrading their knowledge and skills[4].

The role of women in Brunei Darussalam is significant as they play a major part in contributing not only towards their families but also to the country's development. As a mother, women play the main role of instituting in their children good values and manners, shaping them to be individuals who will constantly uphold good morals and ethics and to shun away from immoral activites[5].

Education for Girls/ Women: -

The constitution provides for free and compulsory education for all children between the age of 5 to 16 without sex discrimination. Malaysia, English and Chinese are the three official languages of instruction. In addition to the government schools, there are private Muslim and Chinese schools, operated by religious institutions, however generally all follow the same government developed curriculum[6].

The government has focused great attention on education in general and girl's education in particular. In Brunei Darussalam formal primary education for girls started in 1930 with only 24 students. In 1954 the number of girl students rose from 200 to 500[7].

The government not only provided books to the students but also food. It also provided financial assistance to girls who drop off after 4 years. New schools for girls were started. The enrollment for primary education for girls (2011) was 93% against 92% for boys[8].

The secondary education for girls began in 1954 with 15 students. In 1957 the first ever Secondary School for Girls opened. The girls outnumbered boys. The percentage of girls in 2018 was 94.67 and for boys 92.43%[9]. Tertiary education is offered at both public and private institutions of higher learning. As of 2018, there are several Higher Education institutions in the country. The total enrollment figure for 2017 is 12,135 with 4896 (40.3%) male students and 7239 (59.7%) female students.

The gender gap in academic achievement in Brunei Darussalam becomes apparent at the tertiary level of education. One of the reasons for the gender gap is differences in career interests, with the majority of male school leavers opting to join the security services (police, army & prison department). Secondly, female students outperform their male counterparts in key subjects, such as mathematics and English, which are among the admission criteria of colleges and universities in Brunei. Areas where male used to dominate are now overtaken by females. In the last intake around 65 to 70% of the engineering courses were taken by females[10].

The positive effect of the education policy is evident in the sharp rise in the number of literate women (99.79% for Female and 99.64% for Male in 2018) and in the increase in the number of women in the labor force.

Women have attended high positions in various professional fields such as medicine, law, education, business and engineering. The World Economic Forum (WEF) report noted that Brunei has some of the best educated female citizens in the world[11].

Brunei is a former British protectorate and even today the British influence remains strong in education. Education standards are high in the tiny oil-rich state of Brunei where GDP rose by 226% in the last 10 years. Brunei has the second highest human development index in South East Asia.

Brunei Darussalam clinched the top spot globally in the category of female enrollment in secondary and tertiary education according to the World Economic Forum (WEF) latest Global Gender Gap Report[12].

Political Rights of Women: -

Brunei is not a democratic state. There are no political parties and hence citizens do not have political rights. There is no gender discrimination the constitution is gender-free and women enjoy equal rights with men in all fields like education health and employment[13].

Civil and Personal Laws for Women: -

In accordance with the government's interpretation of Quranic percepts, Muslim women have rights similar to Muslim men in areas such as marriage, divorce and child custody. But a detailed examination shows that some time there is a contradiction in the implementation for example the women have the same choice as men, in choosing their spouse but the laws also provide the consent of the guardian for marriage of a Muslim woman. This practice, many times leads to forced marriage which is an offence according to Islamic Family Law. There seems to be an infringement on the basic right of woman to choose her partner[14].

The Family law permits a man to marry more than one wife, provided he obtains a written permission from the court and has a written declaration stating the grounds on which proposed marriage is claimed to be just and necessary. But many a time this provision is misused as no written consent is taken from first wife and no proper maintenance is given to her. In the sphere of divorce also the wife does not have equal rights. It is very easy for husbands to give Talaq (divorce) orally. The only condition is that he is required to register it with court, within seven days. But divorce outside the court is the most common form[15]. Wife can apply for divorce in a court but its registration depends on the consent of the husband, if he doesn't give consent the court cannot take any action. The only alternative for the wife is to apply for Khula, but this also needs husband's consent and if he does not give consent, the court arranges for two arbitrators to continue working out the settlement. It is noted that when wife initiate the divorce process, it is lengthy, tedious and expensive.

Hudud family laws also discriminate against women in practice and implementation. While stoning applies to both men and women in law for crimes of adultery, rape, abortion and insulting the Prophet Mohammed (S) the experience of other countries with similar laws reveal that women disproportionately bear the brunt of punishment for crimes involving sex and are at a higher risk of being guilty of adultery and extra-marital affairs due to discriminatory policies[16].

Women also face great difficulty in collecting the necessary evidence to prove rape, as they must provide four pious male witness who will testify that they saw penetration occur. If a woman cannot find four men, she can be accused of the crime of Zina (extra-marital sex) punished by death by stoning or flogging of 100 lashes. The rape is unlikely to occur in open hence is impossible for women to prove rape[17].

Abortion in Brunei is largely illegal with an exception if a women's life is in danger otherwise there is severe punishment for abortion. But the couple have the right to decide the number, spacing and timing of their children and have access to contraceptive devices and methods through the government and private clinics. This is an appreciable step as many Muslim countries do not encourage the use of family planning techniques, resulting in fertility and rapid increase of population which is against the interest of not only the country but world at large.

Brunei movement towards stricter Islamic practices initially included measures such as banning the sale of alcoholic beverages and requiring that Muslim children receive religious instruction. Courts for Islamic Law (Shariah) also functions to help Muslims settle personal matters such as marriage disputes. In October 2013 the government announced plans to expand Shariah, to include criminal offences by Muslims. The first of its three phases cover crimes with lesser punishments such as fines and prison sentences for offences such as families who do not observe the fast during Ramadan.

The Second phase, covering crimes penalized by corporal punishments such as whipping or amputation for theft was delayed after international backlash. The final phase covered crimes with severe punishments such as stoning for adultery or sodomy and the death penalty for insulting the Quran. Both the second and the final phase were to be implemented from April 2019, but there has been a lot of criticism against this step by the international bodies.

Economic Participation of Women: -

The country's overall gender equality ranking moved up 10 positions in 2015 to 88 from 98 out of 142 countries[13]. The Global Gender Index 2015, ranked the economies according to how well they are leveraging their female talent pool, based on economic, educational, health-based and political indicators. The Sultanate scored exceptionally well in economic participation where it was ranked 23 as compared to 36 in 2014[14], when women have attended high positions in various professional fields such as medicine, law, education, business and engineering. The participation of women in the workforce increased from 59% to over 70%.

The women in Brunei Darussalam have a very significant role to play in the country's economy. As there is no discrimination either in the field of education or employment women in the last few decades have achieved great success in both the fields. In the field of education, women have surpassed men. This has resulted in a dramatic increase in the participation of women in the labor force, working in professional technical, managerial and administrative jobs from a rate of only 20% in 1971 to 59% today. Brunei women constitute about 49% of the civil services force where they occupy 28% of Division posts[18].

Women today serve in a variety of capacities ranging from entrepreneurs, lawyers, pilots and fire fighters. Women have entered into many male-dominated fields such as the army and the police. Women also occupy important decision-making posts.

An important change was brought in December 2008 prior to which all non-graduate women officers and workers in the public service were upon marriage, relegated from "permanent appointment" status to "month to month" status which meant they were not entitled to benefits similar to their counterparts. This discrimination has been removed, and now all women officers and workers in the public service have permanent appointment status. Today women have a share of 55% in the civil service and 33% in the private sectors[19].

The Brunei Darussalam has been ranked 76th out of 135 countries in the Gender Gap Index 2011. The economic participation of women in the labor force is 62% as against 78% of male participation. Women legislators, senior officials and managers have a share of 35% as against 65% of male personnel and women professional and technical workers have a share of 37% as against 63% of male share[20].

In Brunei women have been active in business from the very beginning. Today there is a large number of women entrepreneurs in Brunei, their activities have no longer been confined to business only but have extended to many other areas like consultancy, architecture, legal practice manufacturing etc. Women have responded positively to the government's call to develop the small and medium enterprises (SME) sector as a potential means of diversifying the economy away from oil and gas.

The overall contribution of women in the economic field needs to be appreciated, which is mainly due to excellent performance of girls/women in the field of education and also the government's vision to provide equal facilities and treatment to women in the economic sphere.

Violence Against Women: -

Brunei comparatively seems to be a crime free society. Domestic violence against women is prevalent all over the world, hence Brunei is no exception to it. There is no specific domestic violence law, but care can be taken under certain laws such as women's and girl's Protection Act. Islamic Family Law Order 2010 and Married Women's Act Order 2010.

The law prohibits sexual harassment and stipulates a punishment for imprisonment up to five years and caning[21]. An important step in the process of law enforcement is the induction of women police in the police department by establishing a special unit of women police to investigate domestic violence cases, hence this is an appreciable step. In most of the countries, there is a charge against policemen of their negative attitude towards domestic violence's cases.

A hotline is available to report cases of domestic violence. The government also arranges for counselling for women and their spouses. In 2007 there were 145 cases of domestic violence as compared to 65 incidents in 2000. But it is believed that the increase may be due to the awareness to report [22].

Though there is no specific policy on women, several domestic legislations provide the protection to the rights of women. Protection of Women and Girls against sexual exploitation is covered under the Unlawful Carnal Knowledge Act 1938 and the Women and Girls Protection Act 1972. The Islamic Family Order 1999 relates to Islamic Family Law with respect to marriage, divorce maintenance, guardianship and other matters connected with family life. To protect children below the age of 18 from discrimination, abuse and neglect the Children's Order 2000 was enforced. The Old Age and Disability Pension to all women once they attain the age of 60 regardless of financial status.

Since the Beijing Platform for Action and the Convention on the Elimination of all forms of Discrimination against women, which Brunei acceded to in May 2006, there have been many government and non-government inter-agency collaborations to promote gender equality. A Ministerial level National Council on Social Issues was established in mid-2008. The Community Development Department is also the custodian of two welfare homes especially established for the safety, protection and rehabilitation of women and girls [23].

Conclusion: -

Brunei Darussalam continuous commitment to the development of all sections is provided in the nations "Vision of 2035" which aims towards an educated, highly skilled and accomplished society, an increase in the quality of life and towards a dynamic and sustainable economy. The positive development and continued progress of women can be attributed to the nation's proactive efforts in improving the lives of the people[24].

As in Brunei Darussalam more and more women participate in socio-economic activities, they are also confronted with other problems such as the erosion of the family institution. The challenge which they face is to seek the right balance where everyone, women, men and children can participate equally and fully in every aspect of life. This is not easy to achieve but one in which Brunei Darussalam is determined to succeed[25].

References & Notes: -

1. UNICEF - Brunei by Pushpa Thambipillai - University of Brunei Darussalam. August 2020
2. Brunei Demographics of Brunei Wikipedia
3. History of Development on Muslim Women's Education - By Lilly SizanShamsu.
4. 4. Higher Education Institutions and Systems, Brunei Darussalam. January 2019 - by Wendy Hiew
5. Women on Top in Brunei. By AzlanOthamn (2006)
6. Brunei Darussalam - Education and Literacy UNESCO Institute of Statistics.
7. International Schools in Brunei Darussalam
8. Brunei Top of Worlds in Girl's Education - The Daily Brunei Resources November 12, 2015.
9. Ibid
10. Minister of Culture, Youth and Sport, Hi Awang Mohammad Bin Haji Daud - Women play significant role in Brunei – 2007
11. Brunei Darussalam - Gender Gap Index. 2011
12. Brunei Darussalam - Education and literacy UNESCO Institute of Statistic
13. Brunei Top of World in Girl's Education opp. cited.
14. Ibid
15. HanaffiHitup: Rising Divorce Rate a worrying Trend - Brunei Times April 4th, 2013.
16. Muslim Comprehensive Fact Sheet on Muslim Family Laws Brunei Darussalam 59th CEDAW season October 2014.
17. Ibid
18. Women in Brunei - Wikipedia
19. Brunei Bulletin - The Independent Newspaper in Brunei - March 8th, 2020.
20. Brunei - Wikipedia
21. Ibid
22. Ibid
23. Beijing Declaration and Platform for Action Brunei Darussalam Report.
24. Report on the State of Women's Affairs in Brunei Darussalam 2011 - by Rozan Yunos
25. Ibid

3

The Islamic Republic of Iran

THE ISLAMIC REPUBLIC OF IRAN which is also called Persia is the 18th largest country in the world with a population estimated at 83.99 million (2020)[1]. Iran has the fourth largest petroleum and natural gas reserves[2].

Iran is one of the oldest civilizations in the world dating back to 3200-2800 BC. It is a very diverse country; the largest ethnic groups are the Persians and Azerbaijans. The major part (89%) of the population in Iran is Shia Muslim, 10% is Sunni Muslim and the remaining 1% are Christian, Zoroastrian, Bahai and Jewish. Persian is the official language. Iran has one of the largest refugee populations in the world (more than one million)[3].

The Islamic Republic was created after the Islamic Revolution (1979) ending the monarchy. After the victory of Islamic Revolution, a referendum was held by the interim government to take an opinion on Islamic Republic (March 1979)[4]. On 23 December 1979 the Constitution of Islamic Republic was ratified by popular referendum.

The government of Islamic Republic of Iran is officially a theocratic republic. Its political system has elements of a presidential democracy with a theocracy government by an autocratic system. The 'Supreme Leader', (The Head of the State) is a life tenure post. He is the commander in chief of the Armed forces, the Legislature, the Executive, and the Judiciary system, operates under his leadership.

The Legislature of the Iranian Republic has two houses: the Islamic Consultative Assembly and the Guardian Council. The Assembly (270 members) is a directly elected body. The Guardian Council, that acts in many ways as an upper house of Consultative Assembly, has twelve members, the six are appointed by the Supreme Leader, the other six are elected by the Assembly from among the jurists. In Iran, the head of the government is the President, who is directly elected for a term of four years by the people, he functions as the Executive.

The Status of Women: -

Iran has a long political history and women's rights have changed from time to time, depending on the views and fancies of the ruling party. Today women's rights in Iran are limited as compared to not only the developed countries but also the other Islamic countries of the world.

In Iran, prior to the Islamic Revolution (1979), religion was a private matter. Women had a choice to live as they liked. Women were not required to wear hijab. In 1935, Raza Shah mandated that women should no longer be veiled in public. Compulsory hijab was reinstated for female state employees and by 1983 it was made obligatory for women to wear in all public places[5]. The Guidance Police (Morality Police) was to supervise women's dress code violations and women were punished by way of fine or imprisonment, if they violated the rules.

The Shariah Law was declared the law of the land. A powerful body Guardian Council was formed to examine all the bills passed by the Parliament to ensure that the bills are according to the Islamic laws, if they are not the Council has the right to veto them. After the Revolution, several of women's existing laws which were not consistent with the Shariah laws were abolished, and the new laws curtailing women's freedom were passed.

The World Economic Forum's 2017, Global Gender Gap Report ranked Iran 140 out of 144 countries for gender parity. As reported in the 2017-18, Women, Peace and Security (WPS) Index, Iran ranked 116 out of 153 countries in terms of legal discrimination[6]. The World Bank's database, "Women, Business and the Law " lists 23 restrictions in Iranian law that restricts married women, this includes applying for a passport, travelling outside the home, choosing where to live and being head of the household[7].

There are no laws that restrain gender discrimination in hiring. The WPS, also pointed out that there are no laws that penalize or prevent the dismissal of pregnant women from work[8]. The Iranian civil code confers power on a husband to prevent his wife from taking any job found to be incompatible with the family interests or the dignity of the husband or his wife. Women have no legal protection against domestic violence or sexual harassment.

Nearly four decades have passed since the Islamic Revolution, but the gender discrimination is still a challenging issue for Iran. While there has been considerable improvement in women's rights, especially in the fields of education and financial matters, it is still very difficult for women to reach the higher levels of administrative hierarchy.

Political Rights of Women: -

Women became eligible for the right to vote in 1963, they could also become members of parliament. In 1990 there were only 3 women among 268 members, while today there are 17 members in the Parliament. They are also included in the cabinet, as Ministers, but they were denied the rights to stand for presidency. Their claim was rejected on the grounds that the "law does not approve" of women running for president[9].

Civil and Personal Laws for Women: -

Iran's Civil law in general favors men over women, in many ways. One of the civil laws is regarding the legal age of puberty. In Iran when children reach the age of puberty, they also gain penal responsibility, which means they can be legally tried as an adult. This can be disadvantageous towards girls, as generally girls reach puberty around the age of ten and boys at fourteen. This means that girls as young as ten, can be prosecuted criminally.

As part of The White Revolution, Mohammad Raza Shah, presented the Family Protection Laws. These laws included women's rights to divorce, helped to raise the marriage age for boys and girls, and curtailed the custom of polygamy mandating spousal consent before lawfully marrying a second wife. Under these laws the right to divorce, for women, was granted by allowing women to put an end to marriage, if they were unhappy. The law also gave the women the right to keep custody of children. In addition, it gave women the right to an abortion under certain circumstances such as rape or if the women's life is at risk.

Education for Girls/Women: -

Great importance has been attached to women's education in the Iranian society. Formal education for women began in 1907, with the establishment of the first primary school for girls [10]. Women's education continues to rise with a high speed. In the beginning of Khatami's presidency 95% of girls in Iran attended primary school.

According to the UNESCO world survey at a primary level of enrollment, Iran has the highest female to male percentage in the world [11]. In 1997-98, 38.29% of Iranian women enrolled in higher education. This number rose to 47.2% by 2000. The figures of enrollment continue to rise. Today more than 60% of all university students are women.

Data shows that nearly 80% of Iranian women are literate but only 21% are employed. In contrast, 85% of male are literate and 79% of them are employed. In Spite of all the improvement and advancement in the field of higher education, there are still some undesirable restrictions. For example, it is reported that 36 universities had excluded women from 77 fields of study [12].

The advancement of women's higher education is increasingly viewed with alarm by the Iranian conservative groups. They warned that the large female enrollment could cause "social disparity and economic and cultural imbalance between men and women'[13].

Economic Participation of Women: -

Since 1970, Iran has experienced significant economic and social changes, but women's participation remains to be low, as compared to not only developed but also many Islamic states even though it has increased from 9.1% in 1996 to 14% in 2004 and 31.9% in 2009. The official statistics reported by the Census Bureau admits that women's labor force participation remains quite low[14]. The ILO data suggests that female unemployment has been considerably higher than men in recent years. Moreover, women are mostly concentrated in typically female jobs of teaching and caring.

According to the International Labor Organization, the top three areas of female employment are agriculture, manufacturing and education. Great disparity exists as Iranian women do not have even the minimum rights at the workforce. Though Iran is a member of the UN Commission on the Status of Women (CSW) yet it has not adopted any of the CSW recommendations to improve women's economic empowerment[15].

In Iran domestic violence is regulated by the Civil Code, Art. 1105 reads "in relation between husband and wife, the position of the head of the family is the exclusive right of the husband." The Iranian society believes that men are responsible for their household affairs, especially treatment of family members, and would not be subject to intervention by the government[16]. The Census Bureau in Iran has precluded international organizations from conducting studies on violence against women including domestic violence[17]. However, crimes are widespread in Iran. They take place in all kinds of families from different social classes and educational backgrounds, but there are no reliable statistics on it. There is evidence that sometimes girls/women are pressurized into committing suicide so that no one will be punished for their deaths[18].

In Iran the Islamic Penal Code does not criminalize honor crimes. Honor killing can however be prosecuted under the IPC, as murder but in line with Islamic principles there are possible legal mitigations, the IPC reduces the punitive measures for father and other family members that murder children in honor killings[19].

Rape is common all over the world and hence Iran is no exception to it. But there are no official statistics on the number of reported rape cases. Rape is probably the only crime in which in most cases the victim not only feels ashamed but may even be blamed for the incident, for in most of the cases the victim prefers not to report the case in order to avoid public humiliation. In addition, the police also attempt to downplay the number of reported rape cases. Sex outside marriage is prohibited in Iran, as it is against the Islamic principles. This makes it very difficult for girls, who have been raped by their boyfriends to come forward and file a case of rape against them. Iranian society greatly values the virginity of an unmarried girl and losing her virginity before marriage is considered a disaster for the girl and her family.

In a statement on the occasion of the International Day for the Elimination of Violence Against Women, CHRI noted that women in Iran are being subjected to serious and sometimes fatal domestic violence at alarming rates without any effective means of protection, the government takes no effective action despite its obligation under international law to do so.

Iran is one of the six countries in the world which has not yet ratified the convention on Elimination of Discrimination Against Women (CEDAW). Nevertheless, Iran's commitment under other international conventions require the government to take clear steps to prevent violence against women[20].

Iran has made a 20-year Law of the Economic, Social. and Cultural development for the period of 2005-2025. One of the objectives of the plan is to make fundamental changes in the domestic field. But its main focus in these plans is on the status of women, not on the prevention of violence against women. Despite the various legislations and the efforts made by the government, violence against women is still a subject of great concern. One of the problems is the lack of information about these laws and procedures to be followed, by women and the law enforcement agencies. Secondly there are more avenues available to women after the crime is committed, rather than on the prevention of crimes.

It appears that Iranian society is not very clear about its national policies. While on the one hand it claims to be an Islamic state and declares Islam as state religion, on the other hand, many of its laws are contrary to the Quranic principles e.g., Art. 1105 of the Civil Code says "the relations between husband and wife, and the position of the household of the family is the exclusive right of the husband." The Quran does not discriminate on the basis of sex; it has given equal rights to husband and wife. Many women today suffer with normalized patterns of coercion, physical violence and marital rape. It is high time that the government should try to overcome these loopholes.

It appears that the Iranian government does not have a clear vision about the development of the country. While it invests on the education of girls/women it does not utilize the knowledge and talents of its 50 %of population, thereby it is a great loss not only to women but also to the national economy. It is the result of its confused policy towards the role and status of women in the Muslim world.

References & Notes

1. Iran. Wikipedia
2. Ibid
3. Iran Population 2020- World Population Review - 2/17/2020
4. Government of the Islamic Republic of Iran – Wikipedia
5. Ibid
6. Klugman, Jeni (October,2017) Women Peace & Security Index 2017-2018 Report.
7. Women, Business and the Law Gender Equality. Women Economic Empowerment: World Bank Group 2019
8. Klugman, Jeni. Opp. cited
9. Tohid, Nayereh (October 2016) Women's Rights and Feminist Movement in Iran - International Journal of Human Rights.
10. Glavine, Chris (February 6th, 2017) History of Education for Women in Iran
11. UNESCO World Survey 2012
12. Women's Rights in Iran – Wikipedia
13. The Educational Status of Iranian Women before and after the Revolution. English. Khamenei's February 11/2016
14. Tohid, Nayereh (October 2016) Women's Rights and Feminist Movement in Iran. Opp. Cited
15. Women are Force for Change NCRI Women Committee November, 2019
16. Domestic Violence in Iran – Wikipedia
17. Mordig, Azad, Domestic Violence Against Women. Single & Married Women in Iranian Society 2009.
18. Country Policy and Information. Note Iran: Honor Crimes against Women version. October 2017.
19. Ibid
20. Center for Human Rights in Iran - Iran must pass legislation to Protect Violence Against Women November 23, 2018

4

Indonesia

INDONESIA IS AN ARCHIPELAGO COUNTRY of 17000 to 18000 islands stretching along the equator in South East Asia. The country's strategic sea-lane position fostered inter-island and international trade. It has a diversity of cultures, ethnicities and languages[1]. It has more than 300 ethnic groups that speak hundreds of different languages.

Indonesia has the largest Muslim population of the world, approximately 225 million Muslims, but it is not an Islamic State, constitutionally it is a secular state whose government recognizes six formal religions[2].

Indonesia was a former Dutch colony which became independent in 1945. It framed its constitution with a Presidential form of government. The political reforms of 1998 changed Indonesia as a democratic country. Direct presidential elections have been conducted since 2004.

Indonesia is a multicultural society though 99% of its population is Muslim but it has a deep impact of its traditions and culture based on different religions like Hinduism and Buddhism. It does not represent a very strict interpretation of Quranic laws. The rules and regulations differ from place to place depending on local traditions and customs.

The Status of Women: -

It is not easy to describe the status of women in Indonesia due to its cultural and religious diversity as well as the fact that the archipelago comprises tens of thousands of villages spread across thousands of islands, poses complex challenges when it comes to women's rights and gender equality. In many rural and semi - urban areas poverty levels are high and educational levels are low and entrenched cultural beliefs keep women isolated inside the house and out of public life. Hence with such a complex situation, it is very difficult to project the status of women in a condensed and concise manner.

Political Rights of Women: -

Women's suffrage was never an issue in Indonesia, the constitution gave them equal rights with men in politics, although in practice politics is still a male dominated field. Since 2003 every political party in Indonesia was required to include at least 30% of women in their organizational structure at the national level, but this requirement was never fulfilled. In 2004, women had 11.24% of seats in the House of Representatives. In 2009 it increased to 18%. In 2019, there were 97 women in Parliament which amounted to 17.32 %[3].

Indonesia had the first and the only female President Megawati Sukarnoputri from 2001 to 2004. Apart from her there were also quite a few powerful female ministers like Sri Mulyani Indrawati - finance minister, who was voted 'Best Minister in the World' in 2018. Susi Pudjiast the maritime and fisheries minister was notorious for her tough stand against illegal fishing activities[4]. Indonesia's new parliament in 2019, elected Puan Maharani as the speaker of the House of Representative.

Indonesia's second President and dictator, Suharto ruled the country for almost 32 years and increased the inequality gap between men and women during his reign. But now the President Joko Widodo has made gender equality a cornerstone of his agenda during his presidency and is currently a global ambassador for the # He or She campaigned and made his mission to fill his cabinet with strong, smart and capable women.

The above analysis shows that there are great variations in the involvement of women in the political field. To accept a female as the President shows that there is no gender bias, but at the same time there is hardly any political awareness especially in the remote rural areas.

Civil and Personal Laws for Women: -

The civil and personal laws for women differ greatly from place to place, depending on the local customs and traditions. Even though it has Muslim majority but there is no strict implementation of Shariah Law except in a few places like Aceh.

In Indonesian culture, it is the responsibility of the husband to look after the economic needs of the family. However, it is normal for women to pursue economic activity. In most parts of the country Indonesian women traditionally enjoy a degree of social and economic freedom[5].

The practice of child marriage, polygamy, female genital mutilation and other forms of gender-based discriminations are often legitimized by religious interpretations. In many parts of Indonesia local laws compel women and girls to wear hijab, especially in schools and government offices[6].

In Indonesia, child marriage is very common, even though the 1974 Marriage Act, sets the minimum age of marriage for girls as 16 years. UNICEF reported that 14% girls get married even before they are 13 years old. The root of the problem lies in the age-old cultural practice. Though Dowry is rarely practiced in Indonesia, bride and bridegroom prices are practiced in some parts of the country. High fertility rate is a major problem in Indonesia. Traditionally people view children as a source of fortune, and the use of contraceptives is against the religious and moral values. Thus, this contributed to a very high fertility rate.

It is believed that this growing population is a major factor in creating widespread poverty[7].

Education for Girls/Women: -

In Indonesia all citizens must undertake twelve years of compulsory education. Though it has almost universal primary enrollment but at the junior and secondary levels enrollments are slow. Legally the Indonesian women have equal rights to the access of education, however, in practice and in reality, women's rate of participation in all levels of education is far lower than that of men (A Human Development Report (UNDA) 2015) As per the census of 2010, the percentage of women obtaining higher education is 6.62% compared to 7.12% of men. The UNDA report of 2015 shows that only 39.9% women actually complete their secondary education as compared to 49.2% of men[8].

In the field of higher education only 7% of women graduate continue their education to Master's degree and only 3% of them go to doctoral degree education[9]. It is high time that authorities should concentrate more on women's higher education.

Economic Participation of Women: -

The Global Gender Gap Report (2014) prepared by the World Economic Forum, identified inequality in economic participation and opportunity for women as the most significant gender inequality challenge for Indonesia[10].

The Indonesia economy has undergone dramatic changes in the last few decades, yet one area which has not changed is the participation of women in the labor market. Indonesia was ranked 88th out of 144 countries in the World Economic Forum's 2016 Gender Gap Index.

Today apart from agriculture, women are making headway in the non-agricultural sector also, 33% of women work in non-agricultural, male dominated fields like medicine, engineering, architecture[11].

The data reveals substantial variation in gender balance in Indonesian Civil Services, which ranges from 0.00 to 0.83. The National Government Departments with the highest proportion of women are Indonesia National Military Headquarters (0.83), National Agency of Drug & Food Control (0.72) and Ministry of health (0.61)[12].

Most of the top government and private positions are held by men and there is a great difference in the pay between men and women. In the 1970s, when foreign investors began investing in Indonesia it opened wide gates for women workers. From 1990 many women were forced to go to foreign countries like Saudi Arabia, Malaysia and Taiwan as house maids. This indicates the lack of employment opportunities for women in Indonesia.

Violence Against Women: -

Southeast Asia has one of the highest records of gender-based violence in the world and Indonesia was recently ranked as the second most dangerous place for women in Asia, Pacific[13].It is true that Indonesia has high rate of violence against women, but it is difficult to get an accurate picture due to lack of authentic information. This was mainly due to lack of reporting mechanisms available to the victims of violence and also that discussing sexual violence is a label that prevents women from reporting.

The first reliable nation-wide survey on gender violence was conducted in 2017, by the Indonesia Ministry of Women and Child Protection and the United Nations Population Fund. The Report said that there was a 25% rise in violence compared to 2016(from 259, 150 to 348, 446 cases). But speaking on International Women's Day, the Minister Mariana Amir Uddin pointed out that the rise may not necessarily indicate an increase in cases but it could be that more women are willing to come forward to report the cases[14].

The Report revealed that Indonesian women most frequently face abuse behind closed doors, in the form of domestic violence and dating violence which accounts for 71% of cases. Of the reported cases in a private sitting, 41% involved physical abuse, 31% sexual abuse, 15% psychological abuse and 13% economic abuse. Among the 26% of violence cases occurring in a public place most took place in schools, places of work and neighborhoods [15]. The Commission pointed out the lack of safety for girls and women.

To conclude, it may be pointed out that Indonesia has achieved success in the economic field and is a good example and experiment of a pluralistic society, where people of different ethnicities live, a place for respect for diversity, and could find abundant opportunities to prosper. However, in spite of all this, women have remained without their share of respectfulness and have to struggle to live and get their valid share in the overall development of the country.

Shamim Aleem

References & Notes: -

1. Population by Region & Religion 2010 By Penduduk Menurut, Wilayah Don Agama Yang Dianut
2. Ibid
3. Women in Politics in Indonesia-Asia Sentinel. December 19, 2018.
4. Gitija House- How Women are Transforming Indonesia-Gatka Bharadwaj, 2019.
5. Harsono, Andreas (25 November 2014) Opinion, Indonesian Women's right under serge.
6. Zahra, Tri Inaya. "The implementation of CEDAW Related to Women's Quota in Indonesian Parliament - December 2016.
7. Social & Demographic Issues in Indonesia- Future Directions International (2011)
8. Gender Bias and Indonesia Education System - Aquarin Priyantna - 17 June 2016.
9. Ibid
10. Abstraction-Indonesian Partnership for Economic Governance- Monash University- June 2017- A study of Gender inequality in employment.
11. Indonesian World's biggest Muslim Country puts more Women into senior-roles-The Straits. 25 July 2017.
12. Mapping Indonesian Civil Service, The World Bank Group-2018 characteristics of Indonesia's Civil Service.
13. Chatham House opp. Cited
14. Ibid
15. Ibid

5

The Republic of Maldives

MALDIVES IS A SMALL ISLAND nation in South Asia, located in the Arabian Sea. It has a chain of 26 tolls comprising a territory of 298 km² (115 sq mi) [1]. It has a population of 515,696 inhabitants. It is one of the smallest Asian countries. Many islands are far and disconnected from the capital city and the population is scattered.

Maldives is a very ancient country. It is difficult to trace its history of the ancient period. Buddhism probably spread in the 3rd century BC. At the time of Asoka there was a 1400-year long Buddhist period [2].Maldives culture developed during this time. In the 12th century, Islam reached the Maldivian archipelago. There is an interesting story, how Maldives was converted into an Islamic state. According to local folklore a Moroccan merchant Abu Barakat Al Barbara, visited the country, Abu Barakat found that a sea demon named Ranna-mauri was terrorizing the people of Maldives. Locals believed that the demon could be pleased by the sacrifice of a virgin girl. A young girl would be chosen to be sacrificed and left in a cave overnight and the next day she would be found dead.

Abdul Barakat suggested that he would be able to get rid of the sea demon by reading the Quran in front of it. The King desperately promised to convert the Maldives to Islam, if Abdul Barakat could get rid of the sea demon for good. The merchant accepted the challenge and instead of putting the girl in the cave overnight, he placed himself. When the sea demon appeared, he recited the Quran and according to some versions, the demon then fled in terror and did not appear again. The King fulfilled his promise and ordered the entire nation to embrace Islam. After Abu Barakat's death he was buried in a tomb which remains as a symbol of gratitude even today[3].

From the 16th century the region came under the influence of European colonial power, with the Maldives becoming a British protectorate in 1887. In 1965 it became independent and a presidential republic was established in 1968[4]. But the government did not have smooth sailing, the political instability continued and added to it were drastic effects of tsunami in 2004-2005. Only nine islands escaped from flooding, while fifty-seven islands faced serious damages[5]. Maldives continues to face the struggle for power. In 2018, Ibrahim Mohammed Salih won the election and became the president of Maldives.

The President is the head of the State and government. He appoints the cabinet, after the approval by People's Majlis (Parliament). There is no separation of powers. Maldives has 26 natural atolls. They are scattered and their connection with the center is very difficult[6].

Maldives has enormous quantities of cowry shells (an international currency in the early days), fisheries trading local goods such as coir rope and coco dimer (Aakash) are the main source of revenue.

The Status of Women: -

The status of women in Maldives was traditionally fairly high. The kinship system on the island is patriline. However, there are accounts of writers dating back to the 14th century when Queens are recorded among the earliest rulers in the islands[7]. Maldivian society takes great pride in its uniqueness and it is generally influenced by traditional values such as performance for the extended family. Respect for parents and elders are very important values.

The small island of Maldives is an example of a Muslim country where women have until recently enjoyed a modest freedom due to their relatively moderate form of Islam. But in recent times, Maldives has been influenced by some Islamic countries like Saudi Arabia and Pakistan which has made Maldives a more conservative country. Women lost many of their rights after Mohammed Nasheed came into power as a president in 2008. But after the recent election (2018) with Ibrahim Salih as president a positive change in favor of women is expected. He has recently appointed two women as Supreme court judges (against which there was a lot of criticism) and announced six months of maternity leave to women employees. [8]

Political Rights of Women: -

As per the Constitution (2008) the Maldives is a Sovereign, Independent Democratic Republic based on the principles of Islam. The Constitution (Art.17) guarantees gender equality and assures that there will be no discrimination on the basis of sex.

The political suffrage was given to women by the Constitution of 1964 and the literacy criteria as a qualification for voters was removed in 2008. Women were earlier not allowed to contest for presidency but now they are permitted to do so. But on the whole women's participation in parliament remained very low. The International Parliamentary Union places Maldives at 136th rank out of 154 countries (only 5 female MPs out of 85 members, which amounts to 5.88%) [9].

Civil and Personal Laws for Women: -

Like many other Muslim countries Maldives is also governed by two sets of laws, the common law based on the British model and the Islamic Shariah law. In Maldives Shariah law prevails in the judiciary.

The Maldives family law is very simple. It deals with subjects like marriage, divorce, child custody etc. The minimum age of marriage for girls is fixed at 18 years, but the court can grant permission for the marriage of a girl under 18 years. This provision has given a loophole and child marriage is common [10]. Polygamy is permitted. A male can marry up to four wives. He has to apply to court, the only condition is his financial position to support his wives, consent of his first wife is not required. This has given a free hand to men to marry up to four wives, which is a clear violation of the conditions of marriage as laid down in the Quran.

Husband and wife both have the right to take divorce. The man can give divorce orally by pronouncing Talaq, but in view of the growing number of divorces in Maldives which is the highest in the world (touching 11% where the world average is between 3 to 4%), it has been made obligatory to get it through the court [11]. There is no lengthy procedure, it is very easy for the husband to give divorce to his wife. He does not need to pay any alimony to his wife. The wife can also apply for the divorce but many a time the court has asked the wife for the reconciliation and told her to go back and stay with the husband which becomes very difficult. In one case the courts thrice rejected a wife's application for divorce, the fourth time it was granted by the high court. In such cases it is very difficult for women to stay in the house with an unpleasant atmosphere. The wife can take Khula after paying some agreed amount but she does not have any financial claim on her husband's property.

The family law came into effect in 2001, and the Penal code codified Hudud offense and ratified it as late as 2014. Hudud offenses include adultery and fornication apostasy, theft, banditry, consumption of alcohol and slander. They remain as offenses with non-negotiable penalties such as public flogging, amputation and stoning. However apart from public flogging for fornication and pregnancy out of wedlock, other punishments for Hudud offenses are generally not enforced, for want of sufficient evidence. As a result, men often escape punishment while women are convicted. In 2006 almost 80% of flogging punishment for fornication were handed down to women [12].There are quite a few glaring examples of severe punishment mooted out to women. In 2013 a 15-year-old girl had been sentenced to 100 lashes after being raped by her step-father. The sentence was rescinded by International outcry. In 2015, a woman who was convicted of adultery was sentenced to death by stoning[13].

In the Maldivian society husband is the bread earner and women have to take the responsibility of family. The husband does not like to share the household work with women. In a survey it is revealed that hardly 4% of men like to share household work[14]. In the last few decades due to expansion of tourism, men have to go from island to island in search of a job, in the absence of husband, wife has also to be the bread earner along with family responsibilities. In such cases she is crushed between the two roles; as there is not much help by the way of maternity leave plans or childcare centers.

The procedure of divorce for men is very easy but when women apply for divorce, there are a number of obstacles. Many a time the court refuses and asks the wife to go back and live with the husband in the same house. Apart from the financial burden, in the absence of proper shelter houses, it is very difficult for women to stay in the same house. With the easy procedure of divorce for the husband and the provision of polygamy and with a large number of children (a woman, it is presumed marries at least three times in her life time and has minimum of 6 children) with unpredictable child support from the father, a woman has a nightmarish time[15].

A number of surveys have been done in Maldives regarding the role of women in the society. As per the survey of Human Rights Commission of Maldives (HRCM) in 2011 the finding was "our religious beliefs say women were supposed to stay at home". It is believed that men in Maldives occupy the upper echelon of the social hierarchy, women often face subtle and sometimes overt forms of subordination.

In another survey, surprisingly 87.3% of women said "a good wife always obeys her husband even if she disagrees." Of late there seems to be increasing dominance of conservative views about Islam[16].

Education for Girls / Women: -

The Constitution of Maldives guarantees the right to education without discrimination of any kind. Primary and secondary education is not compulsory. There is considerable achievement in the sphere of education. Both primary and secondary education is nearly universal, there is no gender difference. There is a 100% enrollment ratio of girls in primary education. There are 92 boys for every 100 girls in primary education but there are 112 boys for every 100 girls in secondary education [17].

Traditionally, education was the responsibility of religious leaders and institutions. Maldives has three types of schools, Quranic schools, Dhivehi-language primary schools and English language primary and secondary schools. The schools in the last category are the only ones equipped to teach the standard curriculum. There was a dearth of government schools in Maldives in the late 1970s. The Maldives faced a great disparity between the quality of schooling offered in the islands and the Maldives, with the result many mothers had to shift to Maldives for the sake of children's education.

In 1992, the government launched an ambitious project of building one modern primary school in each of the nineteen administrative atolls [18]. The government directly controls these schools.

In 1975, the government with international assistance started vocational training at the vocational training center in Maldives. The training covered subjects like electricity, engine repair welding etc. which were meant basically for male members. The girls were benefited mostly by tailoring centers.

There is very limited scope for higher education in Maldives. Maldives National University was established in 1999, with its main campus in Maldives to provide post-secondary education leading to diploma and bachelor's degrees. It was inaugurated in 2011. Most of the students, for higher education have to go abroad either taking loans or on scholarships. The number of girls getting scholarships is higher than boys, e.g., in 2012, out of 643 students, 359 girls got scholarships as compared to 284 boys [19].

Even though the literacy rate of girls is good, mothers face problems in getting the girls educated. There is a scarcity of good schools and mothers are scared to send the girls to far off places in view of their safety. Maldives is a comparatively poor country so many girls prefer to take jobs after secondary education. Child marriage is another factor that comes in the way of education.

There is a need for good schools for girls in every atoll as Maldives is an Islamic country which believes in segregation and hence the girls separate schools is essential.

Economic Participation of Women: -

Maldives has made considerable economic and political progress achieving five out of eight Millennium Development Goals (MDGs) [20]. Women play a vital role in the social, economic and political fabric of Maldivian life. Their influence is felt from family dynamics to political and private sector leadership. Historically women have always supported the advancement of Maldivian society in a number of avenues from producing the thatch and rope used to construct early houses to raising the country's next generation [21].

Despite the eradication of extreme poverty, the Maldives experiences high levels of inequality with a growing gap between the rich and the poor. Women continue to take the burden of household making it difficult to compete with men in economic and political fields added to it were the natural calamities like Tsunami (2004) making their job more difficult.

Even though the tourism industry is dominating Maldives economy, women have a share of only 4% due to the nature of the job [22]. The demand in the other sectors like fishing has also declined due to the changing nature of the skills needed in the industry now. The impact of all changes has badly affected the women in the labor market which has declined from 42% to 38.2% between 2006 to 2010 [23].

Women mainly work in education, health and welfare sections and their employment in government has expanded. The proportion of women in senior and management positions remains low (10-20%, depending on the industry)[24].The Human Rights Commission (Maldives)states that women's employment is showing a negative trend, the conservative beliefs are fulling an increase in the attitude that women's role in society is to be submissive wives and to raise children[25].

Violence Against Women: -

Gender based violence against women remains an entrenched problem in Maldives. The 2007 study on Women's Health and Life Experiences found that one in three women aged between 15 and 49 experienced physical and sexual violence at some point in their lives[26].

Abuses are carried out in the name of family, religion and culture. Thirty percent of the women justified husband's beating for reasons as trivial as burning the food, arguments, going out without telling him neglecting children or refusing sex[27].

Currently there is no legislation that deals specially with violence against women including domestic violence. There is no legal definition of domestic or family violence[28]. There are a number of international treaties to which Maldives is signatory such as Convention on the Elimination of all Forms of Discrimination Against Women (CEDAW) International Covenant on CEDAW International Covenant on Civil and Political Rights 2006, International Convention on Economic, Social and Cultural Rights2006 and the Convention on the Rights of Child. At the national level the Domestic Violence Act 2012 has made a number of reforms, then there is Sexual Harassment Act 2014.But despite all this advancement a major breakthrough in the prevention and protection of victims of violence and positive progress in the realm of prosecution is yet to come.

The Report of the Special Rapporteur on the independence of Judges and Lawyers (2013) has recommended that Judges, magistrates, prosecutors, lawyers and the police need to be urgently trained on the content of the Act and the procedure of implementation [29].It seems apart from the administrative lacuna, there is a lack of political will, and the casual attitude of the people toward domestic crimes. One of the problems that Maldives is facing in the sphere of law and order is street harassment. According to United Nations Population Fund Activities (UNFPA) Maldives in a survey it is found that 60% of women in Maldives face harassment before they turn 16 years of age, and 40% report being harassed before they turn 10.89% of the victims have never reported harassment to the police. Women find it a part of their daily lives to be harassed on the streets [30].

Though prostitution is illegal in Maldives but government has failed to take proper action, today it is at an alarming level specially child prostitution. Sex trafficking has multiplied after 2004 Tsunami. The main reason of prostitution is poverty. It is more common in poor communities as a last resort of source of income [31].

As per the survey Report of Human Rights Commission of Maldives (2014) there are 1139 female as sex-workers. Studies have shown children as young as 12 are involved in commercial sex, and eight percent of female sex worker was under the age of 18 [32].

The report on the Elimination of Discrimination Against Women (2015) has pointed out the people's attitude towards the domestic crimes. They have the notion that violence against women is mostly a result of women not fulfilling their duty as submissive wives [33].The Report further analyses the reasons for not reporting the crimes to police by victims. "The lack of confidence in the system, fear of intimation, inadequate information on protection measures, stigmatization by the community along with lack of opportunities for economic empowerment are some of the factors that hold the victims from reporting to authorities [34]."

In view of the alarming situation of gender-inequality and people's perception towards violence against women the Commission on Women's Empowerment in Political Process (2014) has recommended the following steps to be taken: -

1. To revise gender messaging in the school curriculum.
2. To conduct gender awareness sensitization programs in schools.
3. Bringing in male and female role models in a wide variety of occupations that break down gender stereotypes.
4. Changing perception and attitudes at every level – which is the most difficult thing to accomplish.

Conclusion: -

Maldives is the smallest Islamic state both by its territory and population. For the past 5000 years, Islam is its state religion, but there is hardly anything which can be called Islamic. Though the constitution does not discriminate on the basis of sex, the way the laws are implemented and the negative attitude of the law enforcement agencies and the public is contrary to the principle of justice and the Quran and sunnah.

The personal law as laid down by Shariah has many loopholes, and at many places is contrary to the Quranic law, e.g. even though polygamy is permitted by the Quran but the essence of the Quran is in favor of monogamy.

Divorce, under the Shariah is permitted but as a last resort. God does not like divorce but Maldives has the highest rate of divorce in the world (nearing 11%). The very concept of family is shattered; women have no respectable place in the society. Domestic violence is the order of the day, people openly acknowledge that men have the right to beat their wives and women are subordinate to men.

It is unfortunate that women themselves have no clear idea about their rights and duties. The bureaucracy has no knowledge and skill about the laws which they are supposed to implement. Hence what is needed is not only to legislate laws, but to create an awareness of this anti-movement attitudes towards women in society.

Maldives is one of the Muslim countries which gives a very gloomy picture of women's rights and status. It is pathetic to note that it was under the Islamic influence for the past fourteenth centuries but they have no idea of Islamic principles. There is clear, discrimination in practically all the sphere of life -family laws, economic indolent of women, job opportunities, violence against women - Women are badly crushed under the wheels of struggle of life [35].It is high time that the government should have a clear policy towards women's rights. There seems to be a lack of political will and weak administrative machinery. There is a need for a drastic change in society's perception about the role of women as they are still guided by the old patriarchal thinking of closing all the doors of advancement for women. The government also seems to be confused about its Islamic policy between the two extreme views.

It is the right time when the International organizations should come to its rescue and help it in changing the status of women.

References & Notes: -

1. The Republic of Maldives – Wikipedia
2. History of Maldives – Wikipedia
3. Women's Rights and the Shifting Tides of Islam in the Maldives, Morocco World News (2017)
4. The Republic of Maldives – Wikipedia
5. Republic of Maldives – Tsunami and its Impact and Recovery (2012)
6. Ibid
7. Country Briefing Paper. Women in the Republic of Maldives 2001
8. Amnesty International Maldives – 2019
9. Women's Empowerment in Political Process in the Maldives 2014
10. Ibid
11. Ibid
12. Maldives Women's Rights – United Nations by Shadiya Ibrahim (2020)
13. The Sun - Paradise Lost. How the brutal regime lashes raped woman for adultery - May 16, 2018
14. Women's Empowerment in Political Process in the Maldives 2014
15. Country Briefing Paper: Women in the Republic of Maldives – 2001
16. Human Rights Council: Report of the Special Rapporteur on the Independence of Judges and lawyers – Gabiela, Knaut. M
17. Girl's Education in Maldives. The Borgne Project Blog – 6/22/2020
18. Maldives Education: 6/29/2020
19. Department of Planning – Statistical year Book 2013 Submission from Human Rights Commission – 2015.
20. Maldivian Women's Rights/United Nations. Opp. Cited
21. Ibid
22. Govt. of Maldives - Ministry of Gender & Family. The Maldives – Study of Women's Health Life Experiences by Emma Fula – 2005
23. Submission of the Report from Human Rights Commission of the Maldives to the U.N. Convention on CEDAW. Committee January 2015.
24. Government of Maldives: Ministry of Gender and Family: The Maldives Study of Women's Health and Life Experiences – by Emma Fula.
25. Report to the U.N on the Elimination of Discrimination Against Women 2015.
26. Maldivian Women's Rights/U. N. 6/25/2020
27. Ibid

28. Government of Maldives: Ministry of Gender & Family Experiences. Opp. Cited
29. H.R. Council – Report of the Special Rapporteur on the Independence of Judges and Lawyers – by GabielaKnaut. 2013
30. International Women's Day (2020). Amnesty International 7/1/20
31. Maldives: The position of Girl's and young Women in Society Report by American University Washington College of Law. 2016
32. Maldives Report reveals Police attitudes to domestic violence/ Asia Pacific Forum. 7/1/2020
33. The Maldives Study on Women's Health and Life Experiences. Opp. Cited
34. Ibid
35. USAID: Women's Empowerment in Political Processes in the Maldives 2014.

6

Malaysia

MALAYSIA IS A COUNTRY IN Southeast Asia. It is the Federal Constitutional Monarchy consisting of thirteen states and three federal territories. Malaysia has its origin in the Malaysia Kingdom. Islam began to spread in Malaysia in the 14th century. From the 18th century it became subject to the British Empire. Malaysia achieved independence on 31st August 1957 and United with North Borneo, Sarawak and Singapore on 16 September 1963 to become Malaysia. Singapore separated from Malaysia on 9th August 1965 and became an independent state.

The country is multi-ethnic and multi-cultural which has a significant effect on its politics. About half of its population is ethnically Malaysia with large minorities of Chinese, Indians and Indigenous people, while recognizing Islam as country's established religion, the constitution guarantees freedom of religion to non-Muslims.

Malaysia is spread over an area of 329, 847 km and has a population of 28,334,135(2010). 61.3% people practice Islam, 19.8%, Buddhism, 9.2% Christianity. 6.3% of Hinduism and 1.3% Confucianism and other Chinese religion[1].

Malaysia is a Federal Constitutional Elective Monarchy the only Federal country in Southeast. The system of Government is closely modelled on the Westminster Parliamentary system, a legacy of British rule. The head of the state is the king whose official title is Yang Di Pertain Aging. The king is elected to a five-year term by and from among the nine hereditary rulers of Malaysian states. The other four states' titular Governors do not participate in the selection. By informal agreement the position is rotated among the nine states. The King's role has been largely ceremonial picking ministers and members of the upper house.

Legislative power is divided between Federal and State legislatures. The Parliament consists of the two houses, the House of Representative and the Senate. The Parliament follows a multi-party system and the Government is elected through a first-past-the-post system [2]. The Prime Minister is the Head of the Executive, chosen by the King from among the elected members.

After independence Malaysian GDP grew on an average of 6.5% per annum. The economy has traditionally been fueled by its natural resources but is also expanding in the sectors of science, tourism and commerce. It has a newly industrialized market economy ranked third largest in Southeast Asia. It is a founding member of Association of Southeast Asian Nations (ASEAN), East Asia Summit (EAS) and Organization of Islamic Cooperation (OIC[3]).

There are 14 states in Malaysia. This means that each of these states is able to enact its own set of laws through the state legislature, governing Muslims in that area. The head of the state (Sultan) in many states is also the head of the religion and the laws require assent of the head of the state.

In 1984, the Federal Parliament enacted the Islamic Family Law (Federal Territories) Act 1984, Many of the states adopted the same version of the IFLA, while several other states adopted their own family law enactments that restrict women's rights in marriage and divorce.

Malaysia operates under a plural legal system based on English common law, Islamic law and Customary laws. The Parliament enacts the majority of laws. These laws are enforced through a Federal judiciary. Islamic laws are enacted by the state legislative bodies and apply only to Muslims. Islamic laws are enforced by Shariah courts that are established at state level. Civil courts have no jurisdiction in matters that fall within the Shariah court jurisdiction. The problem is that Shariah laws in Malaysia differ from state to state as each state has the right to frame its laws and the interpretation of Shariah laws also varies from state to state, hence there is no uniformity of Shariah laws in Malaysia[4].

Political Rights of Women: -

Women in Malaysia have been involved in politics since pre-independence. After the independence the Malaysian constitution granted women the right to vote and to hold office. But the involvement of women in politics was a bit slow. The percentage of women in parliament in 1959 was 3.1% which raised to 3.9% in 1986 and 10% in 2000.

Malaysia is ranked 156th out of 190 countries in terms of women's Representation in Parliament according to the Inter-Parliamentary Union.

In the recent election in 2018 there were 33 women in Federal Parliament (14.9%)[5]. The Deputy Prime Minister is a woman and there are 5 women Ministers and 4 Dy Ministers.

The Committee on the Elimination of Discrimination Against Women in its report (2006) showed great concern about the low level of representation of women in public and private organizations in decision making positions.

The Government is trying hard to enhance the status of Malaysian women by appointing them in important decision-making positions. First time the Chief Justice of Malaysia is a woman. A woman is also appointed as Chief Commissioner of the Anti-Corruption Commission- a post of great significance. The government's efforts to set aside a quote of 30% for women both in politics and bureaucracy, still has not been met.

Economic Participation of Women: -

Malaysia has undergone a remarkable economic transformation in the last fifty years since its independence moving from a low-income agriculture based-rural economy to a middle-income manufacturing and service based urban economy[6].

The transformation of the economy had its deep impact on women's economic participation. There was a gradual increase of the female labor force participation in Malaysia which increased from 44.5% in 1982 to 49.5% in 2012. In 2013 the female labor force participation rate surpassed the 50% mark for the first time and the rate in 2017 reached at 54.7%. But in spite of this increase it was lower as compared to other neighboring countries like Singapore (62.2%) and Thailand (70%)[7].

The government of Malaysia in its Eleventh Malaysia Plan (2016-2020) has targeted an increase in the female labor participation rate to 57% by the year 2020.

In Malaysia there is practically no barrier for females to enter any industry or occupation. Mostly it depends on women's preference. In terms of industry most women are employed in the wholesale and retail trade followed by manufacturing education and food service activities. In 2015, approximately 46% of female workers were employed as service and sale workers as well as clerical support workers. While women in Malaysia enjoy equal opportunity and access to education, they lack behind their male counterpart in economic opportunity.

The Sukkah Report on the Status of Women's Rights in Malaysia 2010 has pointed out the gender pay gap. It pointed out that many women earn less than men for the same jobs of equal value. Although certain jobs require similar skills, qualifications or experience, the pay is less and is undervalued when dominated by women[8].

The Sukkah Report (1999) also pointed out the sexual harassment of women workers. The Ministry of Human Resources introduced a code of Practice on the Prevention and Eradication of Sexual Harassment in the working place. As its adoption was voluntary many employers did not adopt it and those who adopted it did not implement it properly[9].

The Report also highlighted the point that there are more highly educated women than men, but despite their high academic achievement women have to contend with several challenges in the workplace.

The government of Malaysia in 2004, has taken a decision for the implementation of at least 30% of women in decision making positions in the public sector. The government has introduced many initiatives to empower women especially in education and workforce. The government hopes that private sectors as well as the non-governmental organizations will adopt the same policy.

Before the implementation of this policy, the percentage of women in decision making positions in the public sector was 11.8% to 12.9%. After the introduction of the policy, the number of women in decision-making positions in Malaysian public sectors has increased. In February 2010 the percentage increased to 28% in high management positions and 61% in middle management positions [10].

But despite these improvements, women are still facing problems particularly regarding their reproductive roles. A survey conducted by the National Population and Family Development Board (2007) indicates that 67.4% of women respondents have decided to resign due to family responsibilities as they are unable to balance their career and family life [11].

Women join the labor force and dropout during child bearing and child rearing period. This brings us to a very important aspect of national policy. It is not sufficient just to fill the posts with women but to provide those facilities which are essential to fulfill this dual role. Most of the Muslim countries have not given a serious thought to this aspect of the problem.

Education for Girls / Women: -

Great importance is attached to education in Malaysia. There is practically no discrimination between boys and girls. The education at the primary and secondary levels is free for both. The literacy rate has steadily increased to 92% (2008) [12]. Female adult literacy increased from 61.3% in 1980 to 90.8% in 2010(UNESCO, 2016).

The general school enrollment rate is over 92% (2007). The number of girls and boys in both primary and secondary schools are almost equal [13].

Several important reforms took place in the Malaysia educational system which led to increased equality and equity in educational opportunities. In 1970 a significant reform took place in the education system where the Malaysia language was introduced as the medium of instruction in all government schools. The change was also implemented at the tertiary levels. This reform was an important tool to integrate the multi-racial society. The reform increased access to education specially for rural Malaysia whose native tongue was Malaysia language [14].

The gross enrollment in tertiary education increased from 7% in 1990 to 40% in 2009. By 2010 females in Malaysia made up 61.1% of the undergraduates in public universities. Nevertheless, until the 1960s there was a common belief in society in general that women are ideally better off as housewives and when educated should be channeled into teaching, nursing or other famine occupations. The gender stereotyping which affects the student's choice of courses is still prevalent even at the tertiary education level where females are more in the science stream.

Certain courses specially in the vocational and technical fields have been male dominated. Women have been oriented towards service-center courses like teaching, nursing, clerical hotel and catering, tailoring, I.T communication and finance/commerce.

The figures of girls in the field of education are quite impressive but it does not give a clear picture of Muslim girls as 40% of the girls are from other faiths than Islam. The break up figures of Muslim girls are not available anywhere. Hence, the correct evaluation of Muslim girls in the field of education, cannot be made.

Civil and Personal Laws for Women: -

Malaysia introduced a series of law reform to end discrimination against women in family laws, but this only applies to the women of other faiths. In the name of Islam Muslim women not only remain discriminated against, but law reform rolled back rights. They have gained and added further grounds of discriminated [15].

In 1976, the Law Reform (Marriage and Divorce) Act was amended to abolish all forms of discrimination against non-Muslim women. Polygamy was banned. The same rights to enter into marriage and grounds for divorce applied to both men and women. In 1999, the Guardianship of Infant Act was amended to provide for the father and mother to have equal rights to guardianship of their children and the Distribution Act was amended in 1999, to provide for equal inheritance rights for widow and widowers. However, none of these laws were extended to Muslim women. Muslim women in Malaysia face double discrimination - firstly discriminated vis-a-vis Muslim men with IFLA and secondly discriminated vis-a-vis women of other faiths, with Muslim women enjoying far less rights in marriage, divorce, guardianship of their children and inheritance.

In Islam marriage is a contract, where the consent of both parties -bride and bridegroom- is essential but in many places the consent of the Wail(guardian) is also necessary. This provision takes away the girl's right to choose her life partner and turns out to be a forced marriage which is against the concept of Islam.

Though law prescribes the minimum age of marriage for girls as 16, judges can give permission for marriage for girls younger than 16 years, with the result child marriage is very common in Malaysia. In 2012 the courts gave permission to 1,022 applicants out of 1,165 applications for child marriage[16], which amounts to 88% of getting permission.

It is interesting to note that Article 1976 of the Malaysian Constitution banned polygamy for non-Muslim citizens while in the case of Muslims, it is considered a divine right of men and therefore the state has no right to restrict the pratice[17]. The polygamy is allowed with judicial permission. The consent of the first wife is not necessary. The judge takes into account certain factors like financial capacity, guarantee of equitable treatment of co-wives etc. It is reported that to determine illegal polygamous marriages, the court recorded 9,233 cases of prosecution on men accused of committing polygamous marriages without court's permission between 2010 to 2016[18]. This figure was higher than the legal polygamous marriage (8,808) Though there is a punishment for violation of the law, but court takes a very lenient view, the offender pays a small amount of fine and gets the marriage registered.

The husband is supposed to give maintenance to the first wife but there is no way to ascertain that he is doing his duty properly. Muslim men and women do not have equal rights to divorce. Husband can divorce his wife without any condition, while women have very limited grounds for divorce. Moreover, the divorce proceedings are very lengthy and difficult. The divorce rate in Malaysia is very high.

A survey was conducted by Sisters in Islam on the Impact of Polygamy on Muslim Families in Peninsular Malaysia from 2007-2012. It was found nearly 65% of first wives were unaware of their husband's intentions to marry another woman, 40% of husbands reduced monetary contributions to their children and wives. The survey also noted that Shariah courts have not strictly enforced the requirements for polygamous marriages. The rights of Muslim women in Malaysia gives a very gloomy picture. There is an urgent need to see that all reforms introduced by the government to remove discrimination against women, should be applicable to all citizen, Muslim and non-Muslim.

Secondly there is a need to make drastic changes in the Institute of Family Law Arbitrators (IFLA) regarding the women's right to enter into marriage on their own, without the consent of Wali. Amendments are necessary in all the provisions in the Institute of Family Law Arbitrators (IFLA) that respond to a maintenance for obedience legal framework. It is also necessary to make strict rules for polygamy and punishment for violating the rules.

Violence Against Women: -

Malaysia is one of the Muslim countries that has been focusing attention on the issue of gender equality and violence against women. It has taken many initiatives to protect the rights of women and to ensure their safety and security. This is done through establishing and constantly improving policy, legitimate institutional framework and other measures[19].

The Article 8(2) of the Malaysian Constitution was amended in 2001, to remove gender discrimination which was an obligation by the state to achieve its commitments under the CEDAW convention. Another important Act is the Domestic Violence Act (DVA) that was approved in 1994 and executed in 1996[20].

Women were the main objectives of the national policy of the 6th (1991-95) and the 7th (1996-2000) Malaysian Plans, where violence against women was recognized as one of the important subjects. The Malaysian government established a specific Ministry for Women's Affairs in 2001. The Ministry increased its budget from RM 1.8 million (US $ 0.5 million) in 2001 to RM 30.5 million (US $ 8.6 million) in 2005 which was an appreciable step[21]. There were a number of other steps taken by the Ministry such as establishing One-Stop Crisis Centers (OSCC) in all the hospitals in order to support victims of violence. In 1996 it created a system known as "Talien Nur 15999", a 24-hour a day helpline recognized to support early intervention for victims of violence.

Another significant step was providing safe houses for abused females. There are 28 such safe houses run by the Welfare Department. As Family Laws for Muslim women are governed under Shariah, the Islamic Religions Department provides temporary shelters for Muslims survivors of domestic violence. They also provide legal and counselling services to them[22]. Inspite of various attempts made by government, violence against women seems to be increasing as evident from the available data[23].

The Committee on the Elimination of Discrimination against Women in its Thirty-fifth session (15 May-2 June 2006) has made certain comments and suggestions about violence against women in Malaysia.

The Committee expressed its appreciation for state policy but it showed its concern that it did not fully comply with the Committee's guidelines. The Committee recommended that the

State should take immediate provisions for incorporating into national law.

The Committee showed its concern about the existence of the dual legal system of civil law and multiple versions of Shariah law, which results in continuing discrimination against women particularly in the field of marriage and family relations. The Committee was concerned about the State party's restrictive interpretation of Shariah law which adversely affects the rights of Muslim women [24]. The Committee further recommended a strong federal mechanism to put in place to harmonize and ensure consistency of application of Shariah laws across all states.

To evaluate the status and rights of Muslim women in Malaysia is very difficult. Government does not have data based on religion, hence the contribution of Muslim women in any field of activity like education, civil services or economic participation cannot be judged accurately. Secondly Muslim women are denied many family rights which are enjoyed by women of other religions, which is a clear case of discrimination hence it is high time that the government should try to remove these discriminations and make laws which should be applicable to all citizens.

References & Notes: -

1. Religion in Malaysia - Wikipedia
2. Malaysia - Wikipedia
3. Joint Report on Muslim Family Law and Muslim Women's Right in Malaysia - 69th CEDAW Session 2018 - Mussafah
4. Ibid
5. The Star - Women Stamping their mark in New Malaysia's Politics (2019)
6. Women Left Behind Closing the Gender Gap in Malaysia by Beatrice Fuji Yee Lim (2019)
7. Ibid
8. Sukkah's Report on the Status of Women's Rights in Malaysia - 2010
9. Ibid
10. A Gender Quota Policy Implementation and Women Empowerment in the Malaysian Public Sector. By Shariah Syariah, Norcaranes and Marehan Hussain. (2016)
11. Ibid
12. Sukkah's Report. Opp. cited
13. Women Left Behind? Opp. cited.
14. Ibid
15. Joint Report on Muslim Family Law and Muslim Women. Opp. cited.
16. Ibid
17. Ibid
18. Ibid
19. UNICEF – 2009
20. The National Policy of Malaysia toward Violence Against Women - by Bahareh Fellahin - PhD. Student.
21. Ibid
22. Ibid
23. Ibid
24. U.N - Committee on the Elimination of Discrimination Against Women Thirty Fifth Session - 15 May thru 2 June 2006.

7

Morocco

MOROCCO HAS A LONG HISTORY of civilization going back to the Neolithic age (2000 BCE). For some time, it was a part of the Roman Empire and was later home to Islamic and Barbra Empire. Morocco fought in World War II, the French lost control of Morocco and granted it independence on March 2nd, 1956[1]. Morocco has an area of 710,850 km (274460 sq.mil) and a population of over 36 million[2].

Since its inception Morocco has had six constitutions, the first one was in 1962 and the present one in 2011. The Constitution declares, Islam as the religion of the State[3].

The Sovereign state is a unitary constitutional monarchy with an elected parliament. The king of Morocco holds vast executive and legislative powers. Executive power is exercised by the government, while legislative power is vested in both, the government and the two chambers of parliament, the Assembly of Representatives and the Assembly of Counsellors. The King can issue decrees, which have the force of law. He can also dissolve the parliament after consulting the Prime Minister and the President of the Constitutional Court[4].

The Status of Women: -

The history of women in Morocco includes their lives from, during, and after the arrival of Islam. In 622AD as Islam arrived in Morocco the women received their basic rights, under Islam, the right to live, the right to be honored and be respected as Mothers, and the right to own business. From the 1940s until 1956, the Morocco women lived in family units that were" enclosed households" of Harem and where families lived as one unit together and women required permission from the men before leaving the household. The women's main activities during that period were, performing household chores, embroidery and craft, attending Quranic classes and going to a bathhouse known as the Hammam.

Though Morocco has made significant advancements in women's rights since the King Mohammed VI's ascension on the throne in 1999, it still ranked 137 out of 149 countries according to the 2018 World Economic Forum's Global Gender Gap Report and ranked 141 out of 149 countries in Women's Economic participation and opportunity[5].

Morocco's constitutional reforms included several proposals to increase women's political and economic participation. However, women remain under-represented in elected offices and leave school at a younger age than male students[6].

Political Rights of Women: -

The women in Morocco like many other countries, had to struggle hard to fight for their political rights. Women received the right to vote and stand for election in 1963, but it was only in 1993 that a woman was elected for parliament for the first time[7]. A quota system has been implemented at the national level to increase women's representation in the lower House of People.

Women now occupy 35 out of 325 seats in the lower House of People, which amounts to 10.7% seats[8]. After the 2007 elections there was a significant increase of female ministers and women in other positions.

Civil and Personal Laws for Women: -

In the field of Civil and Personal laws there are quite a few landmarks in the history of women's rights. In 1993, the Morocco ratified the treaty on the elimination of all forms of Discrimination against Women (CEDAW) that has proved leverage for further progress in domestic legislation.

Through firm political will, Morocco has also managed to make giant strides towards embodying the principle of gender equality and equity in the fields of family, health, education and employment, as well as promoting women's political representation, and advancing women's active and effective participation in public life[9].

Another significant step in the development of women's rights, was the changes introduced in 2004 in Mutawa, which is the personal status code, or family code. The major provisions in the Mutawa were:

1. Both spouses share responsibility for the family.
2. The minimum age of marriage for men and women was raised to 18 years, unless specified by a judge.
3. Women cannot be married against their will.

A man may only take a second wife if a judge authorizes it and only if there is an exceptional and objective justification for it, the first wife's consent was necessary, and the man should have sufficient resources to support the two families and guarantees all maintenance rights, and equality in all aspects of life. One of the important provisions in the code was with regard to divorce.

Both husband and wife are given the right to file for a divorce. Divorce proceedings take place in a secular court, not before a religious one. The custody of children, first goes to mother than father. The law also provides provision for reconciliation and mediation in order to save the marriage[10].

Most of the provisions of this act were as per the Quranic provisions, but progress for the implementation was slow. One main reason was the lack of awareness of these laws, within the Morocco population especially in the rural areas. The law enforcement agency also did not have a very clear and positive attitude[11].

The 2011, Constitution asserts women's equal rights and prohibits all discriminations. Women's health and social outcomes have improved dramatically. The fertility rate is now one of the lowest in the region. The maternal mortality rate fell by two thirds in just two decades. Girls primary school enrollment rose from 52% in 1991 to 112% in 2012, the highest in the region[12]. The gender gap has also fallen from 41% (1934) to 6% (2012). These developments have not only given confidence to women, but have opened the doors for paid employment.

Education for Girls / Women: -

After Independence girls/women started going to school but they were lagging behind in the field of education. During the regime of king Mohammed VI great efforts were made to improve the situation. The period was known as education decade. The literacy rate increased from 27 % (1999) to 63 % in 2016.But there was a big gap in urban and rural education, almost 90 % of women in rural areas were illiterate.

Efforts were made both by government and voluntary organizations to improve the situation. Mohon Al Omiya (erase illiteracy) was a very popular and a successful project. Morocco also got foreign aid of $100 million, from the US Millennium Challenge Project.

The reasons for the backwardness of women in education were many such as cultural norms, emphasis on gender roles, scarcity of girl's schools, distance and transportation problems.

Economic Participation of Women: -

Inspite of the fact that in the last few decades, Morocco's economy has made appreciable advancement, the women's involvement in formal employment is only 23% (2011). One of the highest figures in the MENA region[13].Women's proportion of the unemployed increased from 25.7% (2002) to 30.6% (2011). Women are heavily concentrated in the textile sector and agriculture.

Morocco has a very large civil service, the share of women is about 39 % but like many other countries, participation at the higher level is weak, not many women are found at the decision taking levels. But in the judiciary women have an important role to play. The first woman judge was appointed in 1961 and by 2015 the percentage of women in judiciary went up to 24%. Women in Morocco continue to face discrimination, poor working conditions, unequal access to training, lower pay and longer hours.

One important factor in the labor market is the employer's perception that women (particularly married women) are less productive. This is compounded by the absence of institutional and legislative support for working women, such as maternity leave or affordable child care[14].

Violence Against Women: -

Morocco is considered as one of the most progressive Muslim countries in the Middle East and North Africa (MENA) region. Yet in spite of amendments made to the family code in 2004, which increases women's rights, domestic violence is still not a crime. Violence against women as in many parts of the world is perceived as a private matter not a structural problem.

Morocco does not provide full protection to women against various types of violence. Although the constitution prohibits discrimination and treatment which is cruel, inhuman, degrading or undermine their dignity but the penal code, does not guarantee the effective protection of women against violence.

Although Morocco is a signatory to the Convention on the Elimination of All forms of Discrimination against Women (CEDAW), the country only recognizes its obligation to eliminate discrimination against women as long as this does not contradict Shariah law[15].

After years of persuasion the law (103-13,) on the Elimination of Violence Against Women was passed in February 2018. The law recognizes some form of abuse including sexual harassment in the public and forced marriage, but the law did not meet the international standard[16].

In spite of its weaknesses the law provides legal protection from acts considered forms of harassment, aggression, sexual exploitation or ill treatment. The new law also provides the way for victims of violence to be offered support, in the form of counselling services and shelters for women and girls victims.

Human Rights published a letter to the government of Morocco in February 2016 demanding domestic violence law reforms following an investigation of conditions faced by women victims of violence in the region.

Rape in Morocco is considered a crime against morality and not against the person. Marital rapes, sexual harassment in public places are not yet offences under the penal code. There is no authentic report on the number of cases of rape in Morocco, but the annual report issued by the King's Attorney General in June 2018, mentions the rape cases as 1600(2017) which is double the earlier number of 800[17]. But the critics say that it does not mean a sudden rise in the cases rather it shows that women are more aware of their rights and are coming forward to report the cases.

In spite of numerous legislations, the political resistance and patriarchal culture stand in the way of implementation of these laws. Some of the barriers include judicial oversight and accountability, police enforcement, judge's discrimination to permit waivers for early marriage and to restrict female initiated divorce. If a woman obtains a favorable resolution there is no guarantee that the decision will be enforced.

The legislation seems to be good but many a times there are loopholes which give discrimination to the enforcing authority defeating the very purpose of the legislation, for example large numbers of girls get married before the age of 18.

It only shows that reforms cannot be achieved only by legislation, it needs the awareness of the public at large and specially of the law enforcement agencies. Another problem is that there is no clear consensus among the people on what they wish the law to be, there is a tussle between the feminist group, Islamists and conservatives who seek to define the modern national identity.

References & Notes: -

1. Wikipedia – Morocco
2. Ibid
3. Ibid
4. Politics of Morocco – Wikipedia
5. News and Information work with USAID-closing Morocco's Gender Gap Gender Equality in Morocco. August 28, 2019.
6. Morocco - MENA Gender Equality profile status of Girls and women in the Middle East and North Africa - UNICEF - 211.
7. Morocco's National Report - Beijing + 10 - Global context.
8. Evaluation of Beijing Platform for Action + 20. -- Excerpt from the Royal Message to the participants of the Third conference on World Politics, October 10, 2010.
9. Mudawaha - from Wikipedia
10. Ibid
11. Morocco - MENA Gender Equality profile 2011. Opp. cited
12. Case Study Summary: Women's Empowerment and Political voice - Morocco April 2015.
13. Ibid
14. Morocco Report on Violence Against Women: Euro Med Rights December4, 2016.
15. Morocco: Report on Violence Against Women: Euro Med Rights - combating Gender based violence in Morocco Kev info - 2017.
16. Why Domestic Violence still plagues - Morocco by Darik Etemadi - 3/20/16.-19
17. The World News June 19, 2018 Annual Report by the King's Attorney General.

8

Federal Republic of Nigeria

THE FEDERAL REPUBLIC OF NIGERIA is a sovereign country, located in West Africa. It has a population of 206 million (2019). It has the 5th largest population of Muslims (50.6%) in the world and 6th largest population (47.9%) of the Christians[1]. It has more than 250 ethnic groups and over 500 languages. English is the official language of the state.

Nigeria gained independence from the United Kingdom in 1960 as the Federation of Nigeria, while retaining the British monarch, Elizabeth II as nominal head of the state and Queen of Nigeria[2].

After the independence, Nigeria did not have a peaceful political environment due to civil war (1966-79) and military rules. On the 29th May 1999, Abdul Salami Abubakar de facto President of Nigeria transferred power to the winner of the 1999 election. A former military ruler General Olusegun Obasanjo, second democratically elected civilian President of Nigeria. This ended almost 33 years of military rule from 1966 until 1999[3].

Nigeria is a federal Republic modelled after the United States Constitution, with a parliament consisting of two chambers. The executive powers are vested in the office of the President, who is elected for a term of 4 years.

There are three sets of laws in Nigeria: -

i. Common law, derived from its British colonial past.
ii. Customary law derived from indigenous traditional norms and practices.
iii. Shariah law used only in the predominantly Muslim states of northern Nigeria.

In most of the Muslim states in Nigeria, Shariah law is a part of civil and personal laws, which generally covers subjects like marriage, divorce, child custody and inheritance. In Nigeria the Shariah law was in existence from the beginning of Islamic state but after 1999, the sphere of Shariah law has been extended to criminal matters also in twelve northern states. The new criminal law concerned about what is called the Hudud offences (i.e. those offences for which specific punishments are mentioned in the Quran) although the Shariah penal codes also include punishments not mentioned in the Quran, like stoning to death. They also include amputations for theft and whipping for zina, alcohol consumption, false witness and other offences [4].

The provisions of the Penal Codes are generally gender neutral. However, there are some exceptions which are generally in favor of men. As in the 1960 Penal Code, the Shariah Penal Codes continue to permit husbands to beat wives. Some of the penal codes (Nigeria, Kano and Bornin, Kabobi states) specify that men's testimony will be worth more than that of women. In the Shariah Penal codes, rape is treated as a form of zina, in the most probable situation of lack of two witnesses, or a confession from the rapist, rape would be hard to prove, and so women would find themselves not only subject to Zina punishment, but also liable for false witness in addition [5]. Thus, the new Shariah Penal Codes deprive women of protection from rape and sexual assaults.

The economy of Nigeria is a middle-income mixed economy and emerging market with expanding manufacturing financial service, communications, technology and entertainment sectors. It is ranked as the 27th largest economy in the world in terms of nominal GDP[6]. But Nigeria has been perverted by political corruption. Nigeria was ranked 143 out of 182 countries in Transparency International 2011 Corruption Perception Index. Nigeria is also a home to a substantial network of organized crime especially in drug trafficking[7].

While Nigeria has made some progress in socio-economic terms in recent years, its human capital development remains weak, the country ranked 152 out of 157 countries in the World Bank's 2018 Human Capital Index[8].

Political Rights of Women: -

Nigeria political history can be divided into three phases:

1. The Pre-Colonial
2. Colonial
3. Post-Colonial

During the pre-colonial period, Nigeria's political structure was purely monarchical. The country was made up of diverse societies and kingdoms. Women participated actively in both the private and public spheres and influenced the socio-political landscape of the various regions. Prior to the advent of Islam and colonialism in north Nigeria women played prominent role in political affair[9]. Thus, it is clear that women were not regarded as subordinate to men, but rather as contemporaries though their rights were limited due to a number of constraints[10]. In the colonial period the women were politically inactive. Europeans considered women subordinate to men, and were not allowed to participate in politics[11]. The western education system benefited men only and very few women could gain access to it. Men had many job opportunities while women were marginalized.

The impact of gender imbalance of the colonial period was carried over into the post-colonial era. While Constitution of Nigeria guaranteed freedom from discrimination, women remained marginalized. This was evident in the composition of parliament in the First Republic (1960-66) where there were only 2 women elected out of 91 in the Senate and two in Eastern House Assembly[12].

In the Second Republic (1979-83) there was only one woman out of 571 Senators and 11women in the 445-member House of Assembly. Even during the Third Republic women's political participation was very low. Only one woman was elected for Senate and a few to the House of Representatives.

The Constitution of the Federal Republic of Nigeria (1999) gave equal political power to men and women but the same thing could not be translated in practice. There was not much improvement in the political participation of women senators in the 109 members of the Senate (1999), the number increased to eight in 2007, but fell down to seven in 2011 and again eight in 2015. Female representation in the House of Representative was equally low, there were 12 Women out of 36 in 1999, 21 in 2003, 26 in 2011 and 19 in 2014[13].

A number of factors are responsible for women's low participation in politics. Nigerian society is predominantly patriarchal in nature where woman's job is mostly confined to household management. She is always considered as subordinate to man. Politics is considered as man's job.

The woman is already overburdened with household work with a large number of children. Then there are cultural and religious restrictions also.

The various surveys conducted by different agencies have shown that public opinion is in favor of the limited role of women mostly confining them in the home.

In Nigeria the family is the main institution of patriarchy. Literally it means the rule of the father, it refers to a society ruled and dominated by men over women. This is inherent in most African families. Giving men a higher social status over females has crept into public life, which reflects in state activities[14].The family plays an important role in maintaining this patriarchal order across generations. The greatest psychological weapon available to men is the length of time they have enjoyed dominance over women, which justifies their subordination to men [15].

Civil and Personal Laws for Women: -

Nigeria is a federation of states and operates under a triple legal system, Federal law, Customary law and Islamic law. Muslims are in a majority in the twelve states of north Nigeria and hence Islamic law is mainly applicable in these states. It generally governs Muslim marriages and family relations. The 1999 constitution of Nigeria gives Shariah courts separate jurisdiction to deal with Muslim personal laws but there is no codification of Shariah laws, hence the interpretation differs from place to place on the whims and fancies of the interpreters [16].

The Penal Code of Northern states of Nigeria bans polygamy (Sec. 370). However, several Nigeria states have adopted their own Shariah based penal codes, which do not have this provision. Muslim men are permitted to have as many as four wives at one time without any conditions or consent of other wives. According to Nigeria's 2013 Demographic and Health survey, 33% men have more than one wife which is the prevailing norm in Nigeria.

Nigeria laws do not prescribe a minimum age for marriage. The child marriage is very common in African states, where the marriage of 7- or 8-years girls is not uncommon. Many times, the age difference between the couple is fifteen years or more. The consent of the girl is not essential, the father or the guardian can sign for her. Many a time this leads to forced marriage, which is against the principle of Islam [17].

In Nigeria it is very easy for the husband to divorce a wife. One divorce process that is occasionally used by husbands is 'sake uku' where the husband pronouns the divorce three times. This process makes reconciliation impossible and the divorce irrevocable.

There are not many divorce cases in Nigeria because of the deep-rooted culture. Most women remain in an unhappy marriage in the interest of their children and fear of the society's ridicule.

The research studies have shown that there is no means by which a woman may divorce a man. If under special circumstances a woman initiates the divorce, the bride's wealth (bride price) paid by the husband at the time of marriage, should compulsorily be returned[18].

The laws pertaining to divorce are openly in favor of man. The woman is placed under such an awkward position that she is practically handicapped and remains as a prisoner throughout her life. There is an urgent need for the Nigeria government to modify its divorce rules and procedure which are against the basic concept of human rights[19].

Education for Girls/Women: -

Nigeria got its independence in 1960 but even today it does not have a sound educational policy and is still lacking behind in the sphere of education. There are a number of factors responsible for this state of affairs. Nigeria has a federal system, under which the responsibility of education is divided between center and states. Moreover, Nigeria right from independence has an unstable government and could not focus on the educational needs of the country. Primary and secondary education is the responsibility of the local governments. The Regional differences in quality curriculum in Nigeria is characterized by the education system. Currently Nigeria has the largest population of out of school learning youth in the world[20].

In 1999, the Nigeria government introduced Universal Basic Education, a program to provide free primary and secondary education for all. But though there has been some improvement in recent years, its results have been limited and Nigeria's educational system still rated very poorly in international ranking[21].

Nigeria, right from the beginning is a patriarchal society where women are always treated as subordinate. In the family preference is always given to the son, in the field of education also girl's education was never a priority. In Nigeria under the Islamic influence, there is a segregation of men and women and hence there was always a preference for separate schools for girls. In the beginning schools were under the voluntary Christian organizations. In 1920 out of a total of 25 secondary schools there were only 3 schools for girls, in 1948 only 8 out of 47 secondary schools were for girls [22]. In 1960 when Nigeria attained independence girl's enrollment figures were very low.

In 1970 the implementation of the free and compulsory Universal Primary Education (UPE) plan was adopted with the help of United Nations Children's Fund (UNICEF) and United Nations Educational, Scientific and Cultural Organization (UNESCO) where more girls were enrolled in the schools. From 1970 to 1994, the enrollment of girls in primary education steadily increased from 30% to as high as 80% [23]. Even then differences exist between enrollment of males and females in all levels of education. The drop out percentage of girls is much higher than boys. In 2010 the female adult literacy rate was 59.4% in comparison to the male adult literacy rate of 74.4% [24].

There are many cultural and socio-economic reasons in Nigeria that prevent women from having access to education. One important reason is the patriarchal philosophy that prefers women to stay home and take care of family instead of attending the school [25].

Another reason is early marriage; 43% girls being married before they turned 18 and 17% before they turn 15 [26]. Some girls are married as early as age 9. Nigeria is a poor country, there are great variations in the different levels of society. Many women take up the trade of providing street food through girls [27]. Girl child labor in Nigeria is the high incidence of girls ages 5-14 who are involved in economic activities outside of education and leisure [28].

The under-graduate figures for women's enrollment rose from 9% (1905) to 25.5% (1974) and 40% in 2004 – 2008 [29]. But the number decreased in post-graduation. The gender disparity was also very glaring in the award of scholarship to girls (10 males to 1 female). Male enrollment at all levels is consistently higher than those of girls [30].

But in spite of all these hurdles educated Nigerian women today are making strides in various professions including non-traditional female professions. The best example is that, the three male dominated professions, the Nigerian Medical Association, the Nigerian Bar Association and the Institute of Chartered Accountants of Nigeria have been led by female presidents[31]. The colonial administration introduced a system of education which mainly emphasized clerical skills for boys and domestic science for girls in the school's curriculum. There are clearly defined gender roles in patriarchy in traditional societies facilitated inequalities in prestige, power and access to resource[32].

In the post-colonial era, the government started to review the old policies. In 1959 Eric Ashby Commission recommended the establishment of Federal Universities and hence five universities were established in 1963[33].

At present there are 302 tertiary institutes in Nigeria 128 Universities- 40 by Federal government and 38 by state governments. There are 50 privates Universities[34]. Though the achievement of Gender equality was not one of the objectives of the government's education policy, but it expanded educational opportunities for women as enrollment for women has increased across all disciplines[35]. The early education curriculum was designed to train women as teachers, nurses and clerks as they were not in medicine, politics, engineering and law. This resulted in shortage of qualified women for top level leadership posts[36].

The Nigerian government of late has taken many steps to improve women's education. The creation of the National Commission for Women, a ministerial portfolio for women's affairs provides additional avenues for the promotion of women's education.

But in spite of all these efforts, the Nigeria women still have poor access to higher education. Nigerian Universities function as major sites for the production and reproduction of contemporary gender identities and gender inequalities[37].

Economic Participation of Women: -

In Nigeria there are great inequalities and discrimination against women in economic field. The basic reason is the structure of patriarchal society, which considers women as subordinate to men. In every sphere of life, the man is the decision maker. Among many tribes in Nigeria it is believed that marriage gives up a woman's right to herself. In practice where bride price is paid, it is common for husband to believe that by paying the bride price, he owns his wife. The act of marriage is seen to give the husband full ownership of the wife[38].

A public opinion poll was conducted by NOI Polls in 2019, to find out the socio-economic challenges faced by women in Nigeria. The findings of the survey were that the poverty is the main challenge but for rural women apart from the poverty, illiteracy, ignorance and lack of social and economic amenities are the main hurdles[39]. 45% of Nigeria's labor force is female. Women's participation in the formal and informal labor market is increasing both in urban and rural areas through the period 1990-2009, but remains lower than that of male[40]. There is an overall increase in female participation from 39.3% in 1990 to 48.1% in 2011[41]. 73.15% of women are involved in farm activities which are primarily production in agriculture, forestry and fishing, 26.85% are engaged in non-farm business activities in manufacturing, sales and services[42].

The number of women who held important elected and administrative positions is extremely low; only 6% of women hold seats in the national parliament[43]. In Federal civil service 227,000 men are employed whereas women's number is only 40,000. Though the number of women in the Federal civil service has increased from 10% in 1990 to 14% in 2005, but mostly it is in the lower grade[44]. Female participation in the teaching profession between 1996 and 2005, rose from 47.6 to 51% at the primary level and from 34 to 36% at the secondary level. At the university level, female participation as academic staff was much lower ranging from 17 to 19% between 2000 to 2004.

The lack of education and child marriage are the barriers to women's employment. The early marriage leads to early pregnancies and health problems. There is no awareness of family planning methods. The lack of government aided child centers creates problems for working mothers.

The Nigerian women are overburdened and crushed in between the two wheels of household and job responsibilities. Many women take up small businesses, which they can operate from home. Urban women sell cooked foods usually by sending young girls out onto the streets or operating small standard this was one of the reasons for not sending the girls to school[45].

As many women in Nigeria find it difficult to take up formal jobs, they prefer to have small business which gives them more flexibility, hence entrepreneurial spirit is strong among women. They account for 41% ownership of micro-businesses in Nigeria with 23 million female entrepreneurs operating within this segment this places Nigeria among the highest entrepreneurship rates globally[46].

Based on the NOI polls survey 2019 it is suggested that the government should adopt a soft loan policy for women to encourage them to start their businesses.

Women smallholders farmers in Nigeria are involved in all aspects of agriculture, yet they are held back by unequal access to resources especially finances. Even though the constitution gives them equal rights but the customs and traditions and even some laws discriminate against them.

The employers (both government and private) should have a well-planned maternity leave plain, flexible working hours and provision for day care centers. It is also necessary for the government to provide vocational training programs for women, to provide employment to them in different fields.

The improvement of the status of women in employment requires action at the national, local and family levels. There must be a change in the attitudes of men and women towards their roles and responsibilities in society.

Violence Against Women: -

A World Health Organization (WHO) multi country study on women's health and domestic violence indicates that in some parts of the world as many as one half of women have experienced domestic violence[47]. In Nigeria domestic violence affects women, irrespective of age, class educational level and place of residence. Nigeria laws and customs categories women as an object who is not quite human.

It is reported that in Nigeria on an average of 300-350 women are killed every year by their husbands, former partners, boyfriends or male relations[48]. Most of the time incidents are considered family feuds, which should be treated within the family. Police generally refuse to intervene and advise the victims to go home and settle the family matters.

The United Nations sponsored Convention for the Elimination of Discrimination Against Women (CEDAW), was adopted by U.N General Assembly in 1979. It calls on governments that signed the treaty to remove all forms of discrimination against women, to ensure women's equal access to political and public life, education, health and employment. In 1979 Nigeria signed the convention and in 1985 ratified it. But in spite of this, one problem which is faced by women is the long technical and cumbersome procedures necessary to enforce these human rights. The legal situation is complicated, In Nigeria international treaties have to be domesticated (enacted internally) before they become part of Nigerian law[49].

In a research study conducted in Lagos and Ibadan, it is found that 40% of urban women have been victims of domestic violence[50]. It is noted that Nigerians do not talk about domestic violence because it seems to be an acceptable part of marriage[51].

The perception of domestic violence in Nigeria varies, based on region, religion and class. All the major ethnic groups in Nigeria have strong patriarchal societal structures that lead to justification of domestic violence.

Domestic violence is widespread in Nigeria and shows no sign of decreasing. The survey conducted by Clean Foundation in 2012 found a wide increase in domestic violence in the past 3 years from 21% in 2011 to 30% in 2015[52].

There is a deep cultural belief in Nigeria that it is acceptable to hit women to discipline a spouse. There is no systematic research on wife beating but circumstantial evidence shows that it is done[53].

Reports of beating, torture, acid attacks and killing of women in the family or relationships are regular features in the media and documented reports.

Human trafficking is another example of violence against women, this is global and Nigeria is no exception to it. Another form of violence which is increasing in Nigeria is acid baths, where the perpetrator throws acid on the victim's body, resulting in disfigurement and possible loss of eyesight[54].

Nigeria is a signatory to CEDAW which recommends that state parties must ensure that legislation on gender-based violence provides adequate protection to all women. Nigeria is also a signatory to the African Charter on Human and Peoples Rights which has been domesticated making the Charter, domestic law in Nigeria[55].

The Charter provides that every individual shall have the right to respect the dignity inherent in a human being and prohibits all forms of exploitation. In addition, the Protocol to the African Charter on Human and Peoples Rights, on the Rights of women in Africa, to which Nigeria is a signatory requires states to enact and enforce laws to prohibit all forms of violence against women.

Unfortunately, Nigeria does not have a law which uniformly provides protection to women against violence. In 2015, Violence Against Persons (Prohibition) Act (VAPP) was enacted which provides protection against a wide range of violence to all not specifically to women only. It was realized that in a strong patriarchal society a gender-neutral approach may be better. Though women are not the direct beneficiaries but it does cover a wide range of violence against women. But much depends the way the Act is implemented by the law enforcing agency.

Conclusion: -

Though Nigeria (specially the northern states) has a Muslim majority population and it was under the influence of Islam from centuries, but it is a sorry state of affairs that it does not have a clear idea about Islamic principles. Many of the laws, traditions and customs are contrary to the principles of the Quran and Sunnah, just to mention a few, the principles of marriage and divorce, and the unequal treatment of women. The government and the people in general also violate the basic principles of Islam, for example the corruption is rampant, there is no transparency. There is a network of organized crimes. It only shows that they have no knowledge about the Islamic values. What is needed is a heavy dose of correct interpretation of the Quran and Sunnah to restructure the society.

One of the biggest problems of Nigeria is its growing population. Nigeria's population increased by 57 million from 1990 to 2008, a 60% growth rate in less than 2 decades as of 2017 the population stood at 191 million[56]. The U.N estimates that the population in 2018 was at 195, 874, 685. By 2100 it is estimated that the Nigeria population will be between 505 million. Nigeria has a poor economy and, if it does not control its growing population, it will not be able to compete with other nations in the race of development. There is a need for a very drastic change in the thinking values and attitudes of the society57.

References & Notes: -

1. A Gordon Nigeria's Diverse Peoples. A References Sourcebook Santa Barbara, California (2003). The World Facebook, Central Intelligence Agency Retrieved 18 July 2019.
2. Ethnicity in Nigeria PBS 5th April 2007, Linguistic Diversity in Africa and Europe - Languages of the World (2011)
3. Nigeria, Wikipedia
4. Women Muslim Laws and Human Rights in Nigeria- Africa program by Ayesha Imam.
5. Ibid
6. Nigeria: Date: World Bank Organization Retrieved 25 May 2020.
7. Nigeria – Wikipedia
8. The World Bank in Nigeria - overview-updated October. 2019.
9. Anyogu and Arinze 2013, Gender inequality and colonization Nigeria in legal perspective.
10. Gender Parity in Parliament, A Panacea for the Promotion and Protection of Women's Rights in Nigeria by Bolanle O Eniolo 2018.
11. Ibid
12. Ibid
13. Ibid
14. Women's Participation and the Political Process in Nigeria: Problems and Prospects - African Journal of International Relations (2010) by Damilola Taiye Agbalajobi
15. Ibid
16. Musawah. Thematic Report on Art. 16 and Muslim Family Law: Nigeria 67th CEDAW Session Genevie 2017.
17. Sexuality and the Marriage Institute in Islam: An Appraisal. Lagos, Nigeria (2005) by Hajiya Bilkisu Yusuf
18. Ibid
19. Danish Immigration Service. Report on Human Rights Issues in Nigeria. Denmark January 2005
20. Abdullahi, Danjuma, Abdullah John (June 2014) The Political will and Quality Basic Education in Nigeria. Journal of Power, Politics & Governance.
21. Center for Public Impact: - ABCD Foundation - case study May17, 2017. Universal Basic Education in Nigeria by Claudia Irigoyen.
22. A Historical Reconstruction of the Colonial Government's Education Expenditure in Nigeria and the place of the Girl - Child 1940-1959. (2015) by Adetunji Ojo Ogunremi

23. Female schooling, Non-Market Productivity, and Labor Market Participation in Nigeria. (2004) by Adebayo Aromolaran
24. Ibid
25. Domestic Violence from Women in Nigeria Wikipedia
26. Women in Nigeria – Wikipedia
27. Give Girls a Chance 5/29/2020
28. Women in Nigeria Wikipedia (2008) by Carter & Togunde
29. Education: A Catalyst for Women Empowerment in Nigeria. Wikipedia (2008) by James A Ojobo
30. Women in Nigeria University system opp. cited
31. Women's Education and work in Nigeria Department of Sociology University of Nigeria. (2009) By Edlyne E. Anugwom
32. Women in the Nigerian University System: Achievements, Challenges and Perspectives by Prof. Olabisi I. Aina
33. Ibid
34. Nigeria Universities Commission NUC March 2014.
35. Women in the Nigeria University system Opp. cited
36. Education: A Catalyst for Women Empowerment in Nigeria - James A Ojobo
37. What can a woman do? Being Women in a Nigeria university by Abiola Odejide
38. Violence Against Women. Journal of Asian and African studies 2005 By Joshua A. Ebigbola, Ambrose Akinlo, Peter O. Ogunjuyigbe
39. Socio-Economic Challenges, Women Face in Nigeria - August 15, 2019.
40. Effect of Education Status of Women on their Labor Market Participation in Rural Nigeria - American Journal of Economics 2014. By O. A. Olowa, A. I. Adeoti
41. Religion and Labor Force Participation in Nigeria, African Journal of Reproductive Health 2016. By Kolawole E. Odusina, Akinwole E. Akintoye, Oluwagbemiga E. Adeyem
42. Gender roles and Inequalities in the Nigerian Labor Market by Sue Enfield- Institute of Development studies 21 May 2019.
43. World Bank SCD 2018.
44. Female Labor Force Participation in Nigeria: Determinants and trends. 2008. By Olukemi I. Lawanson Ph. D
45. Women in Nigeria. Wikipedia
46. Impact of Women on Nigeria Economy. 12/03/2020 PWCN
47. Domestic Violence and Women's Rights in Nigeria. 2009. By Hadiza Iza Bazza.

48. Ibid
49. Ibid
50. Ma Donned (2003) quoted by H.I Raza in societies without Borders 2009.
51. Ibid
52. CLEEN Foundation's National Crime Victimization Surveys. 2013
53. UNICEF. 2001
54. Domestic Violence in Nigeria- Wikipedia
55. Legislation on Violence Against Women: A critical Analysis of Nigeria's Recent Violence Against Persons (Prohibition) Act 2015. By CheluchiOnyemelukwe.
56. Nigeria. Wikipedia
57. Rethinking Global Poverty Reduction in 2019 Booking by HomiKharas, Kristofer Hamel, Martin Hofer

9

The Islamic Republic
of Pakistan

PAKISTAN IS LOCATED IN THE northwest part of the South Asian subcontinent. It spreads over an area of 770880 sq.km (297,638 sq.mi) Geography of Pakistan is a profound blend of landscape varying from plain to deserts, forests, hills and plateaus. The current population of Pakistan is 219,758,134 (March 2020). The urban population is 35.1 %[1]. Pakistan has a multicultural and multiethnic society. Over 96% of the population of Pakistan is Muslim and the remaining 4% is Hindu, Christian and others[2].

Pakistan has a history of over seventy years. It came into existence on 14 August1947 with the division of British India into two nations - Pakistan and India.

This division created a number of problems for the government, where more than six million Muslims were reallocated from India to Pakistan and almost 4.7 million Hindus and Sikhs moved from Pakistan to India. The territorial division created another problem where a part of Pakistan known as Bengal was 1371 miles (2,206 km) away from the main territory of Pakistan, surrounded by Indian continent. In 1971, Bengal rebelled against Pakistan and became an independent state - Bangladesh.

Following Independence, it took nine years for Pakistan to produce the first Constitution in 1956, which was rejected on the final day of its adaptation[3].

In 1973 Pakistan adopted the present constitution known as the Constitution of Islamic Republic of Pakistan. The constitution guaranteed principles of democracy, freedom, equality, tolerance and social justice as enunciated by Islam. The Constitution declared Islam as the state religion of Pakistan.

Pakistan has a federal parliamentary republic where the Prime Minister is the executive head of the government chosen by the people. The President is a ceremonial figurehead.

The Status of Women: -

The status of women in Pakistan greatly differs across classes, regions and the urban/rural dichotomy - especially in those areas which are under the tribal culture. On the whole there is gender subordination of women to men.

It strongly believes in the patriarchal theory, where man is the bread earner and woman the homemaker. This gender division of labor, enforces women to primarily specialize in unpaid care work, as mothers and wives at home. This low investment in women's capital, compounded by negative social biases and cultural practices becomes the basis for gender discrimination in all sphere of life.

In Spite of all-round developments in the status of women, Pakistan ranked 120 among 146 countries in terms of Gender Related Development Index (GRDI) according to the United Nations Development Program (UNDP) 2010 report, and in terms of Gender Empowerment-Measurement (GEM) ranking it 92 out of 94 countries[4].

Education for Girls/Women: -

Education is a major contributor to the social and economic development of the country. It is also a device for bridging the gender gap[5].

Despite the improvement in Pakistan's literacy rate, the educational status of women in Pakistan is among the lowest in the world[6]. The literacy rate for women is 45.8% while for men, it is 69.5%. The literacy rate for urban women is more than five times the rate for rural women[7].

The performance of the education sector in Pakistan is not at all satisfactory. In spite of the provision of free and compulsory education to all children between the age of 5 to 16, a large number of children are not enrolled in schools. The Human Rights Watch (2019 Report) found 25 million children of primary school-age out of school, of which most of them were girls.

There is a great disparity between the education of girls in urban and rural areas. In areas like Khyber Pakhtunkhwa (K.P.K) and Baluchistan the female literacy rate goes as low as 7.2%. Girls face a number of hurdles such as traditions and customs which discourage girls to seek education as their presence is needed at home for household work, scarcity of all-girls schools, long distances to school, problem of transportation and above all security of girls, and fear of attacks on schools by Taliban. After the Taliban took over large parts of the SWAT valley in Pakhtunkhwa in 2007, they started a campaign against girls' education. Over 900 girl's schools were forced to close down and over 120,000 girls stopped attending school[8].

The Human Rights Watch Report: Dreams Turned into Nightmares 2017 focused study on the provinces of Punjab, Sindh and Khyber Pakhtunkhwa (KP). It documented attacks by militants from 2007 to 2015. It is reported that there were 867 attacks in this period. According to the Global Coalition to Protect Education from Attacks, at least 838 schools in Pakistan were attacked between 2009 and 2012. [9]

Malala Yousafzai, the youngest Nobel Peace Prize (2014) winner said that "I was just 10 when more than 400 schools were destroyed. Women were flogged, people were killed. And our beautiful dreams turned into nightmares. Education went from being a right to being a crime. Girls were stopped from going to school." [10]

The government is trying to bridge the gap between urban and rural areas and between male and female education by building

70% of new schools for girls. Girls in urban areas have a better chance of education as there is a gradual change in the thought process of society and there are better facilities like good schools and colleges, transportation and safety of girls.

In the field of higher education there is an appreciable progress in women's education. In 1947 there was just one University in Punjab, now there are 177 universities and degree awarding institutes in Pakistan. The percentage of male students in higher education is 56 %, while for women it is 44 % (2015).

Political Rights of Women: -

The preamble of the constitution of Pakistan supports democratic principles and guarantees fundamental rights to all citizens, without any discrimination on the basis of sex. [11]

Further the constitution authorizes the government to create special laws and rules for specific issues facing women. Article 34, ensures full participation of women in all spheres of national life. Though the women were granted suffrage in 1947, however many women in Pakistan still face social, religious, economic and political obstacles which prevent them from exercising their political rights. Political participation of women in Pakistan's national legislature has never gone beyond ten percent until 2001. This is in spite of the fact that a female Prime Minister - Benazir Bhutto - was twice elected as Prime Minister (in 1988-90 and 1993-96), but this is not an indication of gender equality.

But in spite of these limitations there were appreciable developments in the period between 2008 to 2013, when women were given key parliamentary positions like speaker of the National Assembly. Great impetus was given to women in the recent 2018 general elections, where 105 women were awarded party tickets, while 66 women contested as independent candidates. In the new cabinet of 18 members, 3 are women which is an indication of involvement of women in the decision-making process [12].

Civil and Personal Rights for Women: -

All Muslim countries have a dual system of civil and Shariah laws.

Pakistan is no exception to this; many personal laws are governed by Shariah law.

A Muslim marriage is a civil contract which can be executed and dissolved like any other contract. Both the spouses have the legal rights to dissolve the marriage, however the husband has an inalienable legal right of divorce by pronouncement of Talaq, orally on the other hand wife can only exercise the right of divorce if it is written in her marriage contract, if it is not written then the only way is Khula which also needs the permission of husband and or the judge and whereby she loses her financial rights of Maher and property.

It is a common practice in many places especially in uneducated rural areas to delete the right of divorce from the contract when it is presented to the bride for signature.

Polygamy is legally permitted- a man can marry up to 4 wives-as permitted in the Quran. But some restrictions have been put to restrict polygamy. A man who wishes to marry a second wife is required to obtain the legal consent of his first wife/wives and must have the capability to properly take care of all wives. But here also is the problem of properly administering the law. In many cases the husband can take the written consent of the wife, by using force. Moreover, there is no mechanism to test the equal treatment to wives. The woman has no choice but to submit to his will.

In Pakistan especially in rural and tribal areas, girls get married at an early age. The Pakistani's Child Marriage (Restraint) Act 1929 fixed the minimum age for marriage for girls at sixteen, which was extended to 18 years. The United Nations and other international bodies also recommended that the minimum age for marriage should be 18 years but in spite of this legal restraint the Pakistan has one of the highest numbers of child brides in the world. [13]

In Pakistan Karo-Kari is commonly used as a synonym to honor killing. Karo means "black or blackened man" and Kari is black or blackened woman and refers to sexual relations outside the bonds of marriage. Originally these terms were for man and woman as adulterer and adulteress but now it is used with regard to multiple forms of perceived immoral behavior. Once a woman is labelled as a Kari, family members consider themselves authorized to kill her, in order to restore the family honor.

Pakistan has a patriarchal culture where women are considered as property and they have to live in a very structured society where the chaste and the honor of women are of great importance. Any deviation from the accepted principles of the society amounts to a case of honor killing. The honor killing has also been used to get rid of the wife in order to marry another woman or for women who want to marry persons of their own choice against the family wishes.

In 1999 Amnesty International Report pointed out the failure of the authorities to prevent these killings by investigating and punishing the perpetrators. In 2017, the Human Rights Commission of Pakistan listed 400 cases of honor killing in Pakistan. But these figures are disputed by many. As per Human Rights Watch, NGOs/INGOs the estimated figure is around 1000 honor killings every year in Pakistan. The highest number is in the province of Punjab where in 2014, 7,548 of 10,070 total cases of violence against women were from Punjab. [14]

Rape is common all over the world and woman is not safe in any part of the world. Pakistan has a high rate of rape crime though the accurate data is not available as rape victims have long been silenced due to cultural taboos and culprits often get free. Since 2000, women and girls have begun to speak. A group of activists formed a group War Against Rape (WAR) which created awareness against rape. According to a study by Human Rights Watch, there is a rape every 2 hours, a gang rape every hour and 70-90% of women are suffering with some kind of domestic violence [15]. In a study of female detainees in Punjab (1988) it is reported that around 72% of women had been sexually abused while in custody[16]. In the last two decades there were a number of cases of rape, especially gang rape which focused attention of the public on the seriousness of the problem.

One of the significant cases of rape was of a 30-year-old woman-Mukhtaram Bibi in 2002 who was gang raped on the orders of the village Council as an "honor rape" after allegations that her 12-year-old brother had sexual relations with a woman from a higher caste. Although custom would expect her to commit suicide after being raped[17]. Mukhtaram Bibi stood up and fought the case. In 2014, again a woman was gang raped on the orders of a village Council, from the same village (Muzaffargarh) where Mukhtaram Bibi was raped in 2002.

There are a number of cases where women are raped by police personnel. In 2005 a woman was gang raped by four police officers for refusing to pay them a bribe to release her husband from the prison. A 23-year-old woman in Faisalabad was raped on the orders of the Chief of Police as her husband was arrested for creating forged documents. In 2012 three members of the Border police were charged for raping 5 women[18]. There were quite a few more alarming cases of rape in 2018. A seven-year-old girl was raped and strangled to death in Kasur. In the same year a dead body of a 3-year-old girl was found who was supposed to be raped[19].

Economic Participation of Women: -

There is a broad consensus that no country can progress without the full participation of women in public life. Most of the positive attributes associated with development - rising productivity, growing personal freedom and mobility and innovation - require increasing participation of all groups.

As per the World Bank Report, Pakistan stands near the bottom of women's participation in the workforce. According to the Global Gender Gap Report of 2017, score on the Global Gender index is0.546 with a ranking of 143 out of 144 countries, the labor force participation of females is 24%. About 73% of the total employed women are working in agriculture, forestry and fishing[20].

The World Bank in its Pakistan A 100 Initiative has identified inclusive growth as one of the key factors to the country's successful transition to an upper-middle income by 2047 but this requires women's participation in the workforce to rise from a current 26% to 45%[21].

Even though women's participation in the economic workforce has doubled in the last two decades the progress is very slow to catch up to the world level of 43.9%, the government needs to take steps to address gaps in women's work status to achieve the desired goal.

Opportunities for women civil service aspirants changed at least theoretically after the 1973 Constitution which guarantees equal opportunities for all in services (Article 27) with the government encouraging affirmative action.

In a recent study of the United Nations Development Program (UNDP) (2018). It was pointed out that social barriers remain hurdles in women's representation and advancement in civil service. Though women in Central Superior Services have soared from 9% to 45% over the last 5 years, women mainly tend to concentrate in entry level positions[22]. Gender stereotyping and social norms play a major role in deciding civil service postings.

The report pointed out that in taking forward the Beijing Platform of Action, Pakistan is committed to achieving 30% representation of women in leadership positions. Enhancing women's role in leadership and decision making will thus have an immense impact on gender equality and Pakistan's successful achievement of the Sustainable Development Goal (SDG)[23].

Violence Against Women: -

Violence against women particularly intimated partner violence and sexual violence is a major public health problem and a violation of women's rights in Pakistan. According to 2009, Human Rights Watch, 70-90% of women in Pakistan suffered from some kind of domestic violence and about 5000 women are killed annually[24]. Law enforcement authorities do not view domestic violence as a crime and usually refuse to register a case. In Pakistan each province has its own laws to deal with domestic violence. Article 25 of the 1973 Constitution says that all citizens are equal before the law and are entitled to equal protection of law. There shall be no discrimination on the basis of sex. The constitution also provides the provision that special law can be made for the protection of women.

In 2005, Criminal Law (Amendment) Act was passed to check the inhumane customary practices of the Honor Killings, Sara and Vani[25]. In 2010 the Criminal Law (Amendment)Act made the harassment at the workplace a penal offence. In 2011, the Criminal Law (Second Amendment) aimed at checking the crime of throwing acid on women.

Even though Pakistan has made quite a few laws to protect women against violence and has signed a number of international treaties but in spite of all these efforts it has not been able to reduce violence against women. Human Rights Watch in its Report (2019) found that "Violence Against Women and Girls - including rape, so called honor killings, acid attacks, domestic violence and forced marriages - remains a serious problem" in Pakistan. And the HRW issued a warning over the role of police in sexual violence cases, with officers committing offences themselves and harassing and intimidating those who made obligations[26].

It is recently stated (3/28/2020) that Pakistan will set up more than 1000 Courts dedicated to tackling violence against women in the country. The Chief Justice Saeed Khoza said "these courts will be spread in all districts, they would have a different atmosphere", where victims could speak out "without fear". If this scheme is implemented properly, we can see a ray of hope for victims.

Conclusion: -

It is very difficult to paint a correct picture of the status of women in Pakistan as there are great differences in urban and rural areas, and the progress made in different provinces. The women of the cities of Karachi, Islamabad and Lahore give a very rosy picture of women's development, whereas women of Punjab Sindh and Pankhurst provide a very gloomy picture. It is because of these glaring differences that Pakistan is lagging behind on the world scale. The government needs to focus attention on the needs of women in the rural and tribal areas.

References & Notes: -

1. Worldometer: Pakistan Population (Live) 1950 - 2020. https://www.worldometers.info/world-population/pakistan-population/
2. Demographics of Pakistan - Wikipedia
3. Constitutional History of Pakistan - April 2018
4. Women's Education in Pakistan - Wikipedia
5. June Johnson Lewis (Jan7,2007) Woman Suffrage - Timeline International
6. Women's Autonomy in the Context of Rural Pakistan by Zebra Ayesha Sather, Shahnaz Kasi (2000).
7. Asia's Women in Agriculture, Environment and rural production: Pak (7 February 2007).
8. Pakistan: Attacks on Schools Deva static Education: Human Rights Watch. March 22, 2017.
9. Human Rights Watch - "Dreams Turned into Nightmares" Attacks on Students, Teachers and Schools in Pakistan. 2017
10. Ibid
11. The Constitution of the Islamic Republic of Pakistan. 1973 Article 25
12. Law of Divorce and Khula in Pakistan by Barrister Ali Shaikh
13. We Must Protect our Girls - Sabrina Toppa. Lahore December 2017
14. Honor Killing in Pakistan - Wikipedia 3/31/2020
15. Gosselin Toppi (2009) Heavy Hands: An introduction to the Crime of Intimate and Family
16. Aleem Shamim (2013) Women, peace and Security (An International perspective)
17. Greenberg, Jerrold's:(2010) Marital Rape. Exploring the Dimension of Human Sexuality
18. Khan, Amer Ahmed (2005) Pakistan's real problem with rape.
19. Pakistan: Policemen accused of drunken rape: New Zealand Herald. ATP 22 June 2012.
20. HEAVY HANDS: AN INTRODUCTION TO THE CRIME OF INTIMATE AND FAMILY VIOLENCE BY DENISE KINDSCHI GOSSELIN
21. Sara or Vani is a cultural custom practiced in Pakistan's rural areas especially in Punjab and Khyber Pakhtunkhwa. This custom is practiced to settle crimes like murder or Zina by giving a minor girl in the marriage to a man of the opposite group.
22. Pakistan-court-violence- women CNN.com - June 21, 2019 by Amy Woodyatt and Sophia Saifi

23. Women's Labor Force Participation in Pakistan - by Dr.Aliya Khan(2017)
24. World Bank Blog – Pakistan @100: Shaping the Future 2047. 18th May 2019
25. Major efforts required to enhance Women's representation in Pakistan's Civil Service - Pakistan Today March 3, 2018
26. Remarks made by Jamshed Kasi, the U.N Women's country representative.

10

The Kingdom of Saudi Arabia

THE KINGDOM OF SAUDI ARABIA is spread over an area of 829,996 square miles (2,149,690 square kilometer)[1]. It has a population of about 33 million (33,091,113-2018). 6 million are non-citizen guest workers, Saudi population is 90% Arab, 10% of mixed African and Arab descent, 85% of Sunni's and 10% of Siah[2]. Islam is the state religion, and freedom of other religions is neither recognized nor protected and is severely restricted under the law[3]. Saudi Arabia is an absolute majority, although according to the basic laws of Saudi Arabia, adopted by Royal decree in 1992, the King must comply with Shariah (Islamic law) and the Quran[4]. There is no legally binding Constitution and the Quran and Shariah remain subject to interpretation. There is a Consultative Assembly of Saudi Arabia, known as Majlis-ash-Shura which is the formal advisory body of the kingdom of Saudi Arabia. This body has no executive power. It only has the power to propose laws to the King and his cabinet, it cannot pass or enforce laws. It has 150 members, all of them are appointed by the king. Since 2013, 30 women have been included in it[5].

The Status of Women: -

In Saudi Arabia, women's rights during the late 20th and early 21st centuries were very limited. The provision of Mahram (Guardian) and the ban on driving (since 1980) had severely curtailed the rights. Women were deprived of participation in political, social and economic spheres. The World Economic Forum's 2016 Global Gender Gap Report ranked Saudi Arabia, 141 out of 144 countries' gender parity[6]. The U.N Economic and Social Council (ECOSOC) elected Saudi Arabia to the U.N Commission on the States of Women for 2018-2022. Though it was widely criticized by the international community, it opened the doors for Saudi Women to make advancements in all the fields. The Saudi Arabia started relaxing the rules and regulations that allowed women more independence. Laws concerning justice and criminal procedures, child protection, and abuse have been strengthened, and women were allowed greater access to education, health and mobility. Saudi Arabia also launched an awareness raising campaign to bring attention to women's rights.

Education for Girls /Women: -

One of the main tools for the development of individuals is education. In Saudi Arabia, the main reason for the backwardness of women was the government's educational policy which was different for boys and girls. Girls schooling at all levels - elementary, secondary, high school and university - remained under the department of Religious Guidance until 2002, while the Ministry of education was responsible for boys' education.

The focus on girl's education was to ensure that girl's education did not deviate from the original purpose of female education, to make women good wives and mothers and to do acceptable jobs such as teaching and nursing, that were believed to suit their nature. With the wave of gender equality all over the world, the Saudi Arabia also fell in line with the new trend and had to change the educational policy towards girls.

Though Saudi women have been attending university since 1970 but in the last two decades educational opportunities have grown immensely. Saudi Arabia's first women's university - Princess Nora Bent Abdul Rahman - was founded in 2010. The University is the world's largest women's only university. The university aims to give female students better access to male dominated fields, like computer science, management, and pharmacology.

In 2015, women's undergraduate enrollment surpassed those of men, with women comprising 52% of all university students. Many women's colleges use distance education to compensate for women's poor access to transportation. King Abdullah University of Science and Technology was the first co-educational university opened in 2009.

In the advancement of women's education, one of the great steps was the government funded study-abroad program launched in 2005, sending hundreds of Saudi women to the US, UK, Canada, and many other countries each year7.

Political Rights of Women: -

There is not much scope for political rights in Saudi Arabia as it is, an absolute monarchy where there is no legally binding constitution, the freedom of speech and press is completely curtailed. Elections in Saudi Arabia have been historically rare. Municipal elections were held in 2005 and 2011. The women were granted the right to vote and stand for municipal elections in 2011, and they exercised their vote for the first time in 2015. Saudi Arabia was the last country in the world, to grant suffrage to women (2015). A significant change took place in January 2013, when Saudi Arabia's king Abdullah appointed 30 women to the previously all-male consultative Shura Council (150 members).

Civil and Personal Laws for Women: -

In Saudi Arabia the civil and personal laws are guided by the Shariah, but there is no codification, and the interpretation differs from time to time.

In the last few years, the Crown Prince Muhammed bin Salman has followed a flexible interpretation of Shariah, giving many rights to women specially in the fields of education and workforce. There is no significant change in the personal laws. Marriage continues to be a contract between the husband and wife, but in actual practice it turns out to be a contract between bride-groom and bride's father/relative.

There are no laws defining the minimum age of marriage. Most religious authorities have justified the marriage of girls as young as 9 years. The Saudi Human Rights Commission (2009) has condemned child marriage and has recommended that the minimum age of girls for marriage should be 17 years[7].

Shariah permits polygamy, where a man can marry up to 4 wives at a time, if he can financially support them. He is not required either to take permission from his wife/wives or even to inform them. Over half a million of Saudi men had more than one wife[9]. A woman has no legal avenue to prevent her husband from taking an additional wife, nor to obtain a divorce upon learning of her husband's subsequent marriage.

Man has a unilateral right to divorce his wife without any substantial evidence. The women's rights are limited. She can only take Khula by paying a mutually agreed sum of money to the husband[10].

Economic Participation of Women: -

In the past, women's role in the workforce was very low. Partly it was due to the numerous restrictions (such as guardianship, ban on driving, and segregation at the workplace) on women's freedom, and partly due to the rigid and narrow interpretation of Shariah laws. In 2010 and 2017, the women's workforce was only 18% which increased to 23% in 2010, whereas the world average workforce is 48%.

Although 50% Saudi women are university graduates, unemployment remains high. According to the ILO, labor force participation is lower among women in Middle Eastern and North African countries[11].

Many Saudi women were previously restricted to work in certain fields, such as medicine, nursing and teaching, as there was limited training opportunity for women in fields such as information, technology and management. The lack of these skills hindered women's ability to obtain competitive employment. However, of late more programs in postsecondary institutions have been established in subjects such as computer science, architecture, and law, leading them to gain opportunities to work in different fields.

Saudi Vision 2030 for Women is the recently launched program, committed to increasing the employment rate among women in the near future. The program aims to diversify the economy away from oil and aims towards promoting sustainable changes that can enhance the potential to empower Saudi women to pursue their career goals[12].

Several programs have been launched to empower women economically and help them to secure jobs despite resistance from conservatives, who have been openly assertive against allowing women to work.

Saudi Arabia has recently announced decisions allowing women to apply for jobs in air-traffic control, the traffic police and the military and to positions investigators at the public prosecutor's office. These decisions are made in line with Saudi Vision 2030 to increase women's participation in the workforce from 20 to 30%.

Saudi Arabia has recently appointed princess Reema bint Bandar as the first woman Ambassador to the United States. Saudi Arabia also appointed Amal Yahya Al-Moallimi as ambassador to Norway. Saudi government recently appointed Shaimaa Sadiq Al-Jibran as first female commercial judge[13].

One of the important steps taken by the government is to allow women to work from home and it is expected that it would generate 141,000 jobs. The project has proved very popular especially among women living outside major cities in the kingdom as it provides them with flexible timings and enables them to avoid the challenges of commuting to the workplace. Transport difficulties are often cited among the major factors hindering women from taking up jobs[14].

Under the commencement of Vision 2030, with more women joining the workforce, the unemployment rate for women has significantly dropped. The latest statistics released by Pew Research Center revealed that Saudi Arabia experienced the highest growth rate among G20 countries of women joining the workforce in the past 20 years.

The most recent official statistics revealed that the number of Saudi female workers, in both public and private sectors reached a total of 596,700 in the first quarter of 2019, rising by 282.5% [15]. The ministry also revealed that recently 68 schemes were launched by the government to facilitate employment opportunities for Saudi women, these include schemes like the QARA program, which provides children daycare facilities at workplaces. In the last few years Saudi women are now seen developing professional careers.

Prominent examples include Dr. Salwar Al-Hazzan, head of the ophthalmology department at King Faisal Specialist Hospital in Riyadh, and Luna Olean, as one of the most influential business woman. The other woman who earned the title of first were Arwa-al Hajilij, who was the first female trainee lawyer to be granted an official license from the Ministry of Justice and the first female Saudi police officer was Hajilij. Yasmin Al-Maimane was hired as the first Saudi lady working as a commercial pilot. Saudi Arabia also opened non-combat military jobs for women recently.

Saudi Arabia was one of the few countries in the 2008 Olympics without a female delegation. In June 2012, the Saudi Arabian Embassy in London announced that female athletes would compete in the Olympics in 2012. The Saudi government sanctioned sports for girls in private schools for the first time, prior to this the girls were deprived of sports education in schools.

Violence Against Women: -

In Saudi Arabia domestic violence was considered a private matter. It started receiving public attention in 2011 after a popular television show. Until 2013 violence against women was not treated as a criminal matter. In August 2013, Saudi Cabinet approved of a law, making domestic violence, a criminal offence. In 2008 women's shelters were established in different parts of the country. Some organizations also started education and awareness efforts against domestic violence. In Saudi Arabia there is no penal code and there is no written law, which specifically criminalizes rape or its punishment. Sometimes the rape victim herself is punished due to the negative attitude of law enforcement agencies. To deal with domestic violence, a 24/7 hotline has been set up that operates solely by women, to help female victims of violence [11].

Conclusion: -

Making an assessment of the overall development of women's rights in Saudi Arabia, the Chairman of the Saudi Human Rights Commission has rightly pointed out that the country had experienced a period of great prosperity in line of its 2030 Vision, which contains programs to strengthen and empower women's rights. But Saudi still needs to strengthen its laws especially in the field of personal law on issues like marriage and divorce. There is an urgent need to put a break on polygamy and to provide better avenues for women to take divorce if the rules of marriage are violated.The success of these reforms depends on the positive attitude of law enforcement agencies and the public at large.

References and Notes: -

1. Kingdom of Saudi Arabia- Saudi Arabia// Facts and History by Kallie Szczepanski, (January 2020)
2. Ibid
3. Legal System of Saudi Arabia - Wikipedia
4. Robbers, Gerhard. Encyclopedia of World Constitutions Volume I 2007.
5. Consultative Assembly of Saudi Arabia, Wikipedia
6. Global Gender Gap Index 2016 World Economic Forum. 2016
7. Saudi King: Women will be allowed to vote and run for Office. PBS 26 September 2011.
8. Al-Saheil Turk (13 Jan 2009) Saudi Human Rights Commissions Tackle Child Marriage.
9. Musawah Thematic Report on Muslim Family Law and Muslim Women's Rights in Saudi Arabia. February 2018.
10. Ibid
11. Committee on the Elimination of Racial Discrimination examines the report on Saudi Arabia- 27th April 2018
12. Women's Education the Conversion. March 25, 2009
13. Saudi Vision 2030 for Women in the Workforce- Halima Tahirkheli. 3/07/2018.
14. Drastic Spike in 2019 Saudi Women is joining the workforce in flock - Mariam Nabout- 2019.
15. Women's rights in Saudi Arabia, Wikipedia. 10/20/2019

11

The Republic of Turkey

THE REPUBLIC OF TURKEY WAS founded on the ashes of the Ottoman Empire on 29, October 1923 thus ending 623 years of monarchial Ottoman rule. Mustafa Kamal, the first President of Turkey introduced many reforms to transform the old religion-based and multi-communal Ottoman constitutional monarchy into a Turkish nation state that would be governed as a parliamentary republic under a secular constitution[1]. Between 1923 and 2018, Turkey has been a parliamentary democracy. The presidential form was adopted by referendum in 2017 and the Presidential system came into existence in 2018 giving complete control of the executive to the President and the office of the Prime Minister was abolished.

Turkey is a transcontinental Eurasian country, it's land area, including lakes, occupies 783,356 km (302.4555 sq. mile). It has a population of 80.8 million (2017)[2]. Turkey is a secular state with no official state religion.

There are no official government statistics showing the religious beliefs of the people. A survey conducted in 2016, shows that Islam is the religion of 99.8% of the population with Sunni Muslims as the largest sector, while the 2% are small groups of Christians and Jews[3].

The Status of Women: -

The Republic of Turkey has got exceptional and unique experience on the status of women in the society. These are reflected in the laws, policies and programs followed by the government since the establishment of the Republic of Turkey in 1923. Among the significant laws were the Law of Unity of Education of 1924, which enabled women to have equal educational opportunities with men, and the Turkish Civil Code adopted in 1926, which provided equal rights for women, both within the family and as an individual by completely changing the legal status of women[4].

Another important right which changed the legal status of women was the granting of political rights. Women got the right to elect and be elected in local elections in 1930, and in general elections in 1934, earlier than many of the Western Countries[5].

A number of new legislations to protect women against atrocities in the light of international treaties, such as CEDAW, EU, ILO, OECD, OSCE,[6] to which Turkey was a signatory came into force.

Education for Girls / Women: -

The Constitution has committed to free and compulsory education (for 12 years) to both boys and girls, without any discrimination. As per the data available the female literacy rate has risen to 93.56% and the male literacy rate is 98. 79%. But it is not accurate as it is noted that sixteen million girls have never entered the classroom. This has resulted in a great set back on the involvement of women in the workforce, which is only 39% and Turkey ranked 130 out of 149 on the gender gap index. Illiteracy rate is particularly high in rural areas[6].

There are a number of reasons for the lack of encouragement of girls' education. Child marriage is an important factor, as 15% of girls under the age of 18 years enter into forced marriages[7]. Poverty is another reason, especially with the Syrian refugees in Turkey the parents prefer to marry their daughters to Turkish men. The distance of schools and the question of safety are other factors that come in the way of girls' education.

Turkey's involvement in 2030 Agenda for Sustainable Development aims at eliminating child marriage in the next decade. It also aims at universal primary and secondary education and gender equality. Apart from the government, there are other organizations which are aiming to reduce gender gap in the field of education e.g. CYDD, a non-profit organization is working for girl's education. It has open 50 schools and awarded 100,000 scholarships for girls[8].

Political Rights of Women: -

As mentioned earlier, women in Turkey got the right to franchise as early as 1930. There was a gradual increase in the number of women elected for parliament. In 2015, the number of female Member of Parliament was 98, which amounts to 14.73%, in 2018, the number of elected women in the parliament rose to 104(17.45%). There were two female ministers appointed in the cabinet and five Dy Ministers in the Ministries[9].

Civil and Personal Rights for Women: -

The personal rights of women come under the Turkish Civil Code (2002). The Civil Code upholds equality between women and men and puts an end to sexual discrimination. Many changes are made in the Civil Code from time to time to suit the needs of the day e.g. the earlier version that "The head of the family is Husband, is amended and replaced as "the spouses manage the union of marriage together." The new code makes it specific that the spouses would not require the permission of others in the selection of profession and occupation. This gives more freedom to women to choose their jobs as in many countries the husband's consent is necessary, which restricts the choice of women.

The Turkish Civil Code in 1926, has officially abolished polygamy and made it a criminal act. But in spite of this law, it is reported that a large number of men have a second wife, especially if they do not have a son.

Both the spouses have the right to take divorce. It is recorded that the divorce rate is increasing from 15% to 25% in the last few decades especially among the educated women[10].

The marriage age is fixed at 17 years but judges may give permission of the marriage at 16 year also. It is believed that on an average 28% of Turkish women are married before the age of 18. Because of regional differences in some parts of Turkey like Central Anatolia, 40-50% are married as minors. A report by the Commission on Equality of Opportunity for Women and Men states that childhood marriages are widely accepted by Turkish society.

Economic Participation of Women: -

Women's participation in the labor force and development is an important element of sustainable development. In order to raise women's social status, it is essential to promote their participation into all spheres of life. In spite of the efforts made by the government, the employment rate (for ages 15-64) was 32.2% in 2017[11]. According to the World Bank the labor participation of women in 2018 was 32.7% which does not show a significant change from the earlier records[12]. It may be that this low record is underestimated due to women working in the informal economy. A large number of projects with the help of international agencies have been taken up by the government for the empowerment of women. Despite the relatively low involvement of women in the workforce, women are well represented in other fields like the business world.

The rate of women in the senior level decision-making positions in the bureaucracy is as low as 9.5%, but in the Turkish Foreign Affairs one of the most important areas of bureaucracy and male dominated sphere all around the world, 64 out of 266 are women ambassadors. This shows that women play an important role in international affairs. Women have reached to the highest level of judiciary also were out of 13284 judges 7493 are women [13].

Violence Against Women: -

Women in Turkey enjoy far better legal protections than many of their Middle Eastern Neighbors. Sexual assault and Domestic violence are punishable, and divorce laws give a stake in marital property. But deep-seated, restrictive views of women's role still foment violence and the patchy implementation of existing laws often fails to protect women and girls.

Domestic Violence is common in Turkey. The Ministry of family and Social Policies Report stated that 86% of women in Turkey reported experiencing physical or psychological violence from a partner or family member. Over 300 women died of domestic violence in 2015 [14].

Anti-Violence laws are on the books but the punishment is very lenient. Violence also comes from strangers. In 2019, 474 women were murdered. In the World Economic Forum's Global Gap Index (2018) Turkey ranked 130th among 149 countries much behind its neighboring countries like Tunisia, Algeria and many Arab Gulf countries such as UAE, Kuwait and Qatar.

There were a number of cases of rape and murder by unknown persons. Persons also attack women on their clothing. A journalist pointed out that the perpetrators think that these women deserve to die. When a woman wears a miniskirt, she deserves to get raped. Social taboos obviate justice in many such cases. In many cases the family tries to hide the evidence, as the rape goes against their honor. Even if a case goes to a trial, a judge may lessen a sentence if the woman is deemed to have "provoked" - in clothing, appearance or action - her assailant [15].

Different reports indicate that violence against women increased in the last few years. According to the Women's Rights Watchdog Group "We will End Femicide Platform." Nearly 2000 women in Turkey were killed in 2015.

Honor Killing: -

In Spite of all the efforts taken by the government to combat violence against women, the honor killing is still not being controlled. As per the report compiled by the Council of Europe it is estimated that over 200 women were killed in honor killing in Turkey in 2007[16]. The Turkish Prime Minister's Human Rights Directorate Report of June 2008 stated that in Istanbul, alone there was an honor killing every week, there were over 1000 during the last five years. A report by UNEPA identified the following situations as being common triggers for honor killing: a married woman's extra marital relationship, a married woman getting separated or divorced, a young unmarried girl having a relationship with a male member, a woman being kidnapped and/ or raped[17].

In Turkey young boys are often ordered by other family members to commit the honor killing, so that they can get a shorter jail sentence Forced suicides - where the victim is asked to commit suicide in an attempt by the perpetrator to avoid legal consequences[18]. Honor killing continued to receive some support in the conservative regions of Turkey in spite of the fact that the judiciary in many cases has taken stern actions against the family members.

Turkey is a democratic, culturally diverse country with the inception of the Republic (1923) it enacted important legal reforms to ensure equality between women and men in political and civil rights. Laws were passed to eliminate discrimination against women in 1998. Turkey in order to update its laws with respect to gender equality adopted a number of amendments in the constitution, in 2001, 2004 and 2010 and adopted a new civil code in 2001. Turkey ratified a number of international treaties. It was the first to ratify the Convention on the Elimination of all Forms of Discrimination. Against Women. It was the first country to ratify the Istanbul Convention on Preventing and Combating Violence and Domestic Violence Act. 2011&2012 respectively.

But in spite of all these commitments, Turkey lags behind in gender equality commitment. According to the Global Gender Gap Index of the World Economic Forum (2016), Turkey ranked 130th of 144 countries. It ranked 109th in educational attainment, 113th in political empowerment for women and 129th in economic participation[19].

The question arises why in spite of so many legislation and government efforts, the status of women in Turkey has not come up to expectations. Evidences suggest that the problem lies within the depths of the cultural codes of the Turkish Islamist conservative patriarchal psyche[20].

References & Notes: -

1. Wikipedia of Turkey
2. The Princeton Encyclopedia by Islamic Political Thought - August 2013.
3. Turkish Statistical Institute - Turkey Government - 2018
4. Religion, IPSOS Global Trends (2017) CIA Factbook
5. Republic of Turkey-Ministry of Family Labor and Social Services, General Directorate on the Status of Women - Women in Turkey September. 2019.
6. Ibid
7. CEDAW: U.N Convention on the Elimination of all forms of Discrimination Against Women.
8. Borgen Project: Top 10 facts About Girls Education in Turkey
9. Ibid
10. Women in Turkish Politics – Wikipedia
11. Turkish Television Takes on Topic of Child Brides - New York Times 17th November 2011.
12. The Labor Gender Gap Report 2018 - World Economic Forum
13. Labor force female (% of total labor force)- World Bank - 2018
14. Routine Wealth - Number of female judges and prosecutors in Turkey Oya Armutcu - June 2019.
15. A Chronic problem: Violence Against Women in Turkey by Sarabrynn Hudgins. December 8, 2016.
16. hp//globalrightsforwomen.org/2015/04 legislation is not enough
17. Turkey fails to enforce its Violence-against women laws.
18. Number of Honor Killings in Europe Higher than thought Voanews. com. 23 December 2013
19. United Nations Population Fund publications - 15 Feb. 2015
20. Turkish boys commit Honor Crimes - BBC News 28 Aug 2006.

12

The Republic of Tunisia

THE REPUBLIC OF TUNISIA IS in the Maghreb region of North Africa. It spreads over an area of 163, 610 km (about two-third the size of the United Kingdom.) It has a population of 11,8,619(March 2020)[1], consisting of 98%. Muslims and 2% of Christians and people belonging to other religion[2]. The country has a secular culture where religion is separated not only from politics but also from public life. Tunisia was a French colony which achieved independence in March 1956. President Habib Bourguiba established a strict one-party state. He dominated the country for 31 years[3]. A Revolution took place in 2011, and a new Constitution was adopted in 2014. The Constitution says that the President's religion "Shall be Islam."[4]

The Preamble of the Constitution describes Tunisia as a Republic and Democratic Civil State, based on law, where the sovereignty belongs to the people and the principle of separation of powers is guaranteed. The parliament is unicameral and the President is elected by direct universal suffrage. The first election for the permanent government was held in 2014, Benji Caid Essebsi was elected as the first President of the State.

The Status of Women: -

Tunisia is viewed as a relatively advanced country in terms of women's rights. It is ranked 123rd in the Gender Gap Index of 2014, according to the World Economic Forum, and is therefore one of the highest-ranking countries in the Arab World[5]. Tunisia has repeatedly expressed its willingness to meet international norms and standards with regard to women's rights. the Constitution declared that the State shall commit to protecting women's rights and seek to support and develop them. "The State shall guarantee equal opportunities between men and women in the bearing of all the various responsibilities in all fields."[6]

Politics Rights of Women: -

Women in Tunisia were given the right to vote immediately after Independence in 1957. The new Constitution of 2014, guaranteed equal rights to both men and women, and for representation in all elected bodies. In 2016, Tunisia passed a law, which made it mandatory for all parties to put forward an equal number of male and female candidates[7]. Tunisia is one of the few countries in the world to establish the principle and practice of equal representation of men and women across a candidate list.

In 2018, women occupied 47% of the local council positions; gradually there has been an increase in the number of women occupying parliamentary seats[8]. As of 2017, 73 women were elected to parliament, an increase from 68 in 2016. Today it is the highest in any Arab country.

Civil and Personal Laws for Women: -

Today Tunisia is considered a pioneer of women's rights in the Arab world. The country's Personal Status Code (CPS) is considered one of the most progressive in the region. In 1956, the Code of Personal Status was enacted, but as of today it has undergone many changes. The main provisions under the CPS are: -

i. The abolition of polygamy.
ii. Both spouses have the right to request divorce.
iii. Minimum age for marriage for girls is at 17 years.

iv. Education is made free and compulsory.

v. Same wages for men and women.

vi. Abortion is made legal for social therapeutic reasons.

In 1992, a law was passed under CPS, which provided that the two spouses must treat each other with kindness and consideration, and assist each other in the management of the household and the affairs of their children [9]. This provision replaces the former clause providing that "the woman must obey her husband." [10]

A significant change in the personal law, was brought in 2017, when a decades-old ban, which prohibited Tunisia women from marrying non-Muslim men, was lifted, earlier a non-Muslim man had to convert to Islam before marrying a Muslim woman [11].

Apart from these, women had many other concessions e.g., they could open a bank account and establish business. In 1962, women were able to access birth control much earlier than the women in America. In 1957, the veil at school which was earlier compulsory was forbidden. As the fertility rate was high the government encouraged to limit the number of children. The parents were allowed to have the State benefits up to four children only [12]. The government distributed contraceptive pills, free of cost. the fertility rate in Tunisia has drastically reduced.

Education for Girls /Women: -

Education is given high priority in Tunisia both for male and female. Free and compulsory education is one of the rights guaranteed in the Constitution. The government spends about 20% of its budget on education [13]. About 82% of people over the age of 15, are considered to be literate. Tunisia stands 93rd in the World Bank and has reported that 96.79% of people are literate [14].

Right from the Independence (1956) the first President, Bourguiba gave importance to girls' education. He made girls get rid of their veil. Tunisia has one of the highest female literacy rates among Islamic countries. The literacy rate for females is 96.19.% they have a higher participation rate than males [15].

More girls (81%) are enrolled in secondary schools which is more than their male counterparts i.e. 75%. Although Tunisia girls have a higher enrollment rate, many girl's dropout during or after they complete their primary education. But Tunisia enrollment rates for girls are higher than its surrounding neighbors including Algeria, Egypt, Morocco, Syria, Yemen and even Lebanon and Jordan.

The Statistics show that females are very active in the field of higher education. Young women represent 59.5% of students enrolled in higher education in Tunisia[16]. In the field of higher education women's participation is not only confined to traditional fields of learning like education and medicine but it has extended to the fields of construction, carpentry, black-smiting and heavy equipment maintenance. During the period of 2004 to 2008, the percentage of women in the field of scientific research was 44% to 47%[17].

Economic Participation of Women: -

Though Tunisia is the champion of women's rights especially in the Arab region and has a very impressive record, but in the field of economic participation, its share is very low, just 27.2% in 2012[18]. It is about half the rate of OECD countries. At the same time its female unemployment rate (24 % in 2012) is very high by international standards.

According to ILO data, most of Tunisia female force is found in manufacturing (43%) followed by professional, scientific, and technical/public administration, social security. Human health and social work activities (19.4%), 12.3% in agricultural, forestry and fisheries. 51% are in blue-collar jobs[19].

Despite improved education women's unemployment problem seems to originate on the demand side. Well qualified university educated women have the highest unemployment rate of any group in the population at 47.4% compared to 20.6% among men[20].

The highest female unemployment rates are found in the country's interior. Tunisia's interior lacks the infra-structure, transformation and information network. As pointed out by Ben Salem employed women find it difficult to balance work and family. The Labor Laws differentiate between public and private. E.g. while in public enterprises women get two months paid maternity leave, in most of the private organizations, it is only one month, with certain restrictions. Moreover, there are childcare facilities in public organizations which are lacking in the private organizations[21].

A study on women's and youth Empowerment in Rural Tunisia, pointed out that there is a substantial-discrepancy between what law is and what is practiced, both in public and private life. One of the main reasons for this, is the existence of strong and persistent gender biased norms and attitudes[22]. The report shows that despite many legal achievements, Tunisia still has a long way to go when it comes to women's empowerment.

Violence Against Women: -

Violence against women is a worldwide problem and even the most advanced country like the U.S has not been able to overcome it. Though Tunisia is the champion of the women's rights in the Arab world, but in spite of its bold policies, it still has to go a long way to combat violence against women.

In order to meet its constitution commitment to eliminate violence against women, the government adopted the National Plan for the Elimination of Violence Against Women in 2013. The National Plan aims to end violence against women through the dissemination of information material, the use of free hotline services and by strengthening and increasing access to comprehensive care for domestic violence survivors[23].

In July 2017, The Tunisian Parliament adopted the law on Elimination of Violence Against Women. This is the first law, which recognizes domestic abuse as a crime. The law introduced new criminal provisions and increased penalties for various forms of violence, when committed within the family. It also criminalizes sexual harassment in public sphere. The law requires ministries to provide services to survivors of gender-based violence. The law adopts a comprehensive approach that addresses violence against women through four pillars, Prevention, Protection of women victims of violence, Penalization of perpetrators of violence and procedures, services and institutions that provide support to women victims of violence[24].

The 2017 law also put an end to the marry-the-rapist-law before this law, the Tunisia Criminal Code provided a rapist with exemption to avoid investigations or legal consequences if he married his victim. Laws of this types are historically common and still exist around the globe. But Tunisia took a bold step in repealing this law.

However, despite immense gains on paper, Tunisia women have continued to fight several forms of violence and harassment. According to a 2012 survey of the National Board for Family and Population (NBFP) about one in two Tunisia women had been subjected to violence during their life[25].

It is pointed out by many activists that due to the government's silence on gendered security issues unjust treatment of women still occurs on a daily basis. When a young woman is raped by a police officer for example, she can be charged with indecency which may lead to imprisonment, regardless of her status as a victim[26].

Conclusion: -

There is a great variation in the status of women in urban and rural areas, even though both are governed by the same laws. It is estimated that about 40% of women living in rural areas are illiterate this is in spite of the fact that the Constitution provides for free and compulsory education.

Moreover, these women are not well integrated in the economic and political scene. As recommended in the report of the Gender Election Observation Mission (GEOM) 2014, 300,000 women living in rural areas who have been excluded from the electoral process, need to be given access to vote in future elections in

Tunisia. The fact that these women lacked the official identity card necessary to cast their vote underscore the gap in Tunisia democratic system.

It is easy to pass laws but it is difficult to translate them in practice, keeping the spirit with which, they were made. Even if there is a political will, it may be defeated by the way it is enforced by the law enforcement agencies. This is true, not only in Tunisia but in many developing nations.

References & Notes: -

1. Tunisia - Tunisian Republic County Profile - Nation online project 3/22/2020
2. Tunisia International Religious Freedom Report for 2011. US States Department of State - Bureau of Democracy, Human Rights and Labor.
3. Tunisia- Tunisia Republic opp. Cited.
4. Tunisia Holds First Election under the New Constitution. B.B.C News 26 Oct. 2014.
5. The Situation of Women in Tunisia Gender Concerns International 10/23/2019.
6. 4-way Tunisia is now more progressive than the United States - by Hayes Brown January 27, 2014.
7. 5 Times Tunisia proved it is a Pioneer in Women's rights - Leyla Khalifa 2018.
8. UN Women. Historic Leap in Tunisia women make up 47% Local Government - August 2018.
9. Ibid.
10. Gender Inequality and Economic Inclusion in Tunisia: Key Policy Issues. By Valentine M. Moghadam, Ph.D. 09/03/2018
11. 5 Times Tunisia. Opp. cited
12. Code of Personal Status in Tunisia- Wikipedia
13. Education in Tunisia - Wikipedia
14. Facts about Education in Tunisia The Borgen Report
15. Women in Tunisia - Wikipedia
16. Ibid
17. The Situation of Women in Tunisia. Opp. cited
18. Dynamics of gender In Equality, Women's Labor force participation in Tunisia. Valentine Moghadam, June 2017.
19. Ibid
20. Ibid
21. Ibid
22. ILO Home- Women and Youth Empowerment in Rural Tunisia - An Assessment, using the Women's Empowerment in Agriculture - May 2018.
23. The Situation of Women in Tunisia. Opp. Cited

24. Tunisia Gender Justice - Assessment of Laws affecting Gender Equality and Protection Against Gender- Based Violence - UN Women, UNFPA and ESCWA
25. Ibid
26. Ibid
27. Ibid

PART III

1

The Impact of COVID-19 on Women

THE YEAR 2020, THE TWENTY fifth anniversary of the Beijing Platform for Action - was supposed to be ground-breaking for gender equality, but with the spread of the COVID-19 pandemic, even the limited gains made in the past decades are at risk of being rolled back.

The COVID-19 pandemic has challenged the normative structures and behaviors of almost every country in the world. The data, from many countries show that more men have died with epidemic than women. Even if this finding is correct, women are expected to suffer the long-term consequences of the pandemic as it permeates and changes societies and affects livelihoods and this effect could last up to a generation and will have a disproportionate impact on women[1].

The impact of COVID-19 across the global economy will be profound, markets and supply chains have been disrupted, business are required to close or scale back operations and millions have or will lose their jobs for livelihood. ILO has established that full or partial lockdown measures now affect almost 2.7 billion workers representing around 81% the world workforce.

Emerging trends suggest that women's economic and productive lives will be affected disproportionately and differently from men. Across the globe, women acquire less secure jobs have less access to social protections and are the majority of single parent households. Their capacity to absorb economic shocks is therefore less than that of men.

The situation is worse in developing economies where the vast majority of women, (nearly 70%) are in the informal economy with few protections against dismissal for paid sick leave and limited access to social protection.

As of March 31,2020, 105 countries had passed fiscal response packages equivalent to a total of U.S $4.8 trillion. According to UNESCO, 1.52 billion students and over 60 million teachers are now home as COVID-19 school closure expands.

Coronavirus Cases	
Total Coronavirus cases	101403805
Deaths	2182238
Recovered	73298686
Source: - Worldometer, January 28, 2021	

Economic Impacts: -

Across every sphere from health to the economy, security to social protection, the impact of COVID-19 is severe. The women and girls, who are generally earning less, saving less, and holding insecure jobs, or living close to poverty, are feeling the burnt of economy more.

Apart from women, the pandemic will have a direct impact on young girls with the closure of schools, education becomes inaccessible. With the adverse economic impact on livelihoods and family incomes, there is a danger that could roll back all of the gains made by the U.N. Millennium Development Goal where gender parity up to a high school education was generally achieved across the region by 2015[2].

While reports on COVID-19 reveal the health of women generally is adversely affected due to reallocation of resources and priorities, including sexual and reproductive health services.

The pandemic is deepening pre-existing inequalities exposing vulnerabilities in social, political and economic systems which are in turn amplifying the impacts of the pandemic[3].

Health Impacts: -

Health pandemics can make it more difficult for women and girls to receive treatment and health services. Women and girls have unique health needs, but they are less likely to have access to quality health services.

One very serious concern is the risk or exposure to women due to their nature of work. It is estimated worldwide; women constitute 70% of the health workers and are more likely to be front line health workers, especially nurses, midwives and community health workers. They are also the majority of health facility-staff-such as cleaners, laundry, catering and as such they are more likely to be exposed to the virus[4].

In most of the countries, they are providing care and service physically and mentally around the clock, putting themselves and their families at risk of infection. And they are doing so in a setting where personal protective equipment (PPE) supplies are dwindling. It is reported that in Italy 20% of the health workers were infected with COVID-19 and in Spain it was 14%. In China more than 3300 women workers were infected with COVID-19[5].

The diversions of money and attention from the provision of sexual and reproductive health services may result in excel morbidity, increased rates of adolescent pregnancies, HIV and sexually transmitted diseases.

Unpaid Care Work: -

There are gross imbalances in the gender distribution of unpaid care work. Before this pandemic, women were doing three times as much unpaid care and domestic work as men. In the context of the pandemic, the increased demand for care work is deepening, already existing inequalities in the gender division of labor.

In most of the countries, men are not in the habit of sharing household work. It has become a very serious problem for women who have to go and serve outside (such as healthcare personnel) and also take care of children, husbands and elder persons at home. The working women after their strenuous work are completely exhausted and result in a physical and emotional breakdown.

Violence Against Women: -

With the rapid spread of COVID-19, violence against women and girls are increasing worldwide. Pandemic combined with economic and social stresses and measures to restrict contact and movement has made the situation worse. Crowded homes, substance abuse, limited access to services and reduced peer support are exacerbating these conditions. Many of the women are now trapped in their homes with their abusers.

The correct data on the increase of violence is not available. The numbers reported are likely to reflect only the worst cases. Another serious dimension of this pandemic is that it is being used as a threat to women, abusers are exploiting the inability of women to call for help or escape, women risk being thrown out on the street with nowhere to go[6].

Added to this is the problem of availability of support services which have been drastically cut down and have changed their priorities. Voluntary groups are affected by lockdown or reallocation of resources. Many shelter homes are already full, some have been converted into health centers.

The prioritization of the police and security forces have been shifted towards pandemic problems resulting in the absence of vigilance on domestic violence cases in remote communities.

The Impact of COVID-19 on Women in Middle East: -

With fewer girls attending schools and family income slashed early marriage-already a widespread problem across MENA-is also likely to increase. In addition, violence against women in all its forms is increasing as the pandemic spreads. With lockdowns and curfews, families are forced to spend significant time together. Many husbands and some working wives are out of work increasing stress and tensions as money becomes tight.

Even in countries across Europe; the domestic violence has increased by 24%[9]. Since the COVID-19 the MENA region is not immune to similar outcomes.

Women in Arab region are exposed to conditions that make them more susceptible to contracting COVID-19. Female nurses, midwives and support staff dominate the health-care and social services fields in many Arab countries increases their risk of infection[7].

Financial resources are being diverted towards efforts to contain the spread of COVID-19 making it more difficult for women to access health services, including sexual and reproductive services.

More women are expected to fall into poverty during this pandemic, severely affecting female headed households in the region. The COVID-19 is expected to result in the loss of 1.7 million jobs in the Arab region, including approximately 700,000 jobs held by women. The female participation in the labor market is already weak in the Arab region with high unemployment among women reaching 19% in 2019[8].

Projections indicate that the informal sector will be particularly impacted by the COVID-19 pandemic. Women constitute 61.8% of workers in the informal sector in the Arab region, and will therefore suffer disproportionately.

In the Arab region, nearly half of the female population of 84 million is not connected to the internet nor has access to mobile phones. The illiteracy rate among the women is also high which may affect ability to have access to information about the crisis in terms of prevention response and seeking help[9].

It is predicted that domestic violence is likely to increase in every nook and corner of Arab region because of the forced co-existence, community closures, economic stress, food insecurity, and fear of exposure to the virus.

The pandemic may also make it more difficult for domestic violence survivors to seek and receive help, due to a curve on movement, limited availability of services or lack of knowledge of services. Services for domestic violence survivors such as shelters and hotlines may be strained or deprioritized during the COVID-19 pandemic. Moreover, domestic violence shelters may face overcrowding or closures.

The police and justice systems may deprioritize gender-based violence during this period. This is especially relevant in the Arab region where the majority of countries do not criminalize domestic violence [10].

The Impact of COVID-19 on Women in Africa: -

Although African governments had made notable progress in enhancing women and girl rights. COVID-19 has deepened the pre-existing gender inequalities and exposed them to a series of human rights violations. An upsurge in sexual violence, domestic violence, child marriage and Female Genital Mutilation (FGM) has been recorded in various countries, across Africa [11]. In Kenya, there has been increasing reports of sexual and gender-based violence with cases of FGM and child marriage. In Nigeria there has been a surge in defilement abuse of minor girls, domestic violence and abuse of the rights of widows since a partial lockdown was imposed.

In South Africa, from the first week of COVID-19 lockdown, there has been a spike in gender-based violence with many women and girls trapped at home with their abusers. In Uganda, numerous cases of police brutality have been reported. Access to maternal care has also been curtailed by and several pregnant women are reported to have lost their lives [12].

The Impact of COVID-19 on Women in Southeast Asia: -

The New York Times report has clearly pointed out that the healthcare workers are at the highest risk of being infected by the coronavirus [13]. In Southeast Asia 79% of nurses are women. There is a surge in demand for medical professionals, especially nurses. In Malaysia 3000 retired nurses have come back to join the fight on the frontline. In Indonesia 54% of medical practitioners are women[14]. The role of women as medical practitioners shows the importance of women in fighting an international emergency. As women are putting their lives on the line responding to the coronavirus, the number of domestic violence cases in Indonesia and Malaysia is increasing.

The Malaysian government's crisis hotline, Talien Kasih has received a 57% increase in calls from women since the lockdown was imposed. In Indonesia, the Legal Aid Foundation of the Indonesian Women's Association for Justices, received a threefold increase in the number of reported domestic violence cases, just two weeks after work-from-home, stay -at-home orders were imposed[15]. The sad aspect of this picture is justification by the people of this trend as it is considered to be "culturally acceptable".

The government of Southeast Asia is trying to impress upon the people the intolerance of domestic violence. In Indonesia, the government has launched a mental health hotline service available to everyone In Malaysia the government has reopened the Talien Kasih hotline, which was temporarily closed.

While Indonesia and Malaysia do not have the best gender equality indicators in Southeast Asia, their responses to the rising number of domestic violence cases show that they are acknowledging women's role in fighting COVID-19.

It is pointed out by many that COVID-19 pandemic is causing widespread social disruption and women are bearing the brunt of it. Custody arrangements, financial obligations such as alimony and court closures could disproportionately affect women.

Conclusion: -

Women hold only 7% of the World's government leadership roles, but several women leaders are drawing praise for their skillful navigation of the coronavirus pandemic. In Germany, New Zealand and Taiwan-among other countries-women are being held up as role models on how to effectively guide countries through public health crises. They have been lauded for their swift action, trust in science and ability to make difficult decisions with empathy and compassion. As a result, they have succeeded in minimizing the impact of this disease[16].

Reports from The New York Times, the Washington Post, CNN and USA Today have all highlighted the success of women leaders who have minimized deaths from COVID-19, in their countries by making hard decisions and inspiring the support of their communities[17]. Their approaches have been effective because they incorporate empathy and compassion. These women leaders know how to inspire their population to make the necessary sacrifices to control COVID-19 outbreaks.

The pandemic of COVID-19 has shown to the world that the power of women has not yet been fully tested or trapped. We need to build towards using it more often[18].

It is unfortunate that New Year of 2020.instead of bringing the message of prosperity and happiness turned out to be a year of great stress and strain for the whole world. The corona virus started in China in the last week of December 2019 and by January 2020 WHO declared it a global health emergency. Today (January 28, 2021) 10,140,3805 people are affected by this pandemic and 2,182,238 have lost their lives.

It was only by the end of February or early March that countries realized the seriousness of this disease and started taking serious actions to prevent the disease from spreading -flights were cancelled, shutdowns were declared, schools and colleges were closed down, people were asked to work from home, all public places were closed down. Income was reduced, scarcity of food and essentials increased, hospitals were overcrowded, within a few weeks the life was completely paralyzed lifestyle which people have never seen.

The ordinary citizen has a very bad time. The families were locked into small houses with children and elderly people, the tension and violence increased in the family. Of all the people women have to suffer most. The household work increased tremendously. The quality and quantity of food reduced; many working women have dual responsibilities which badly affected their health.

It is nearly a year now, but there is no sign of improvement, rather the second wave of pandemic is spreading now. The countries have started talking stern actions again. People are in a very helpless position. But in this gloomy atmosphere the only ray of hope is Woman -she has to come forward and face with determination the challenges of life until the things come back to normal.

References & Notes: -

1. U.N Women-Policy Brief the Impact of COVID-19 on Women. 2020
2. Ibid
3. Ibid
4. World Health Day, The Nursing Workforce is critical to COVID-19 and Global Health- Edson Araujo and Alejandra Garcia April 2020.
5. Policy Brief. The Impact of COVID-19 on Women Opp. cited
6. Ibid
7. The Gendered Impact of COVID-19 in the Middle East by Hafsa Halaqa. June 11, 2020.
8. Ibid
9. Ibid
10. U.N Women - The Impact of COVID-19 on Gender Equality in the Arab Region -11/08/2020
11. Women's Rights in Africa- The Impact of COVID-19 on Women's Rights in Africa. 09/04/2020
12. Ibid
13. Australian Outlook - The Disproportionate Effect of COVID-19 on Southeast Asian Women: Case Studies from Malaysia and Indonesia
14. Ibid
15. Ibid
16. Stanford Medicine - Scope. Women Leaders Shine during COVID-19 Pandemic. May 12, 2020 Traci while
17. Ibid
18. Remarked by Sirleaf, a winner of the Nobel Peace Prize in Standard Medicine opp. cited.

2

Conclusion

Introduction

THE WESTERN UNDERSTANDING OF MUSLIM women remains under influenced by evidence from a single region - Middle East and MENA - which does not give a very bright picture of the status of women. The recent research studies reject the idea that the Islamic religion is the primary determinant of the status and conditions of Muslim women. The gender-based inequalities which the Muslims women faced is mainly associated with the so-called patriarchal gender system. The system regardless of religion, features Kin-based extended families, male domination, early marriage (and consequent high fertility) restrictive codes of female behavior, the linkage of family honor with female virtue and occasionally, polygamous family structire[1]. Most research scholars now see Islam as no more inherently misogynist than the other major monotheistic traditions. They agreed to the view that the sacred book (the Quran) and sunnah have been interpreted in ways that support patriarchal social relations[2]. Many cultural practices associated with Islam and criticized as oppressive to women are misidentified as "Islamic" Controversial/practices such as female circumcision, polygamy, early marriage and honor killings are not limited to Muslim population. In my brief study of the status of women in the Muslim world, I found that today

Islam has spread in every nook and corner of the world. In the beginning it mainly spread through the traders coming from the Muslim states. The countries which adopted Islam were already under the influence of other religions like Buddhism, Hinduism and Christianity, with their deep-rooted traditions and customs. Though they accepted the basic principles of Islam, but it was merged into the traditions and customs of that country, resulting into different patterns of Islamic states. A close examination reveals that many Islamic principles were modified to suit the local needs e.g., the strong patriarchal base in many countries (like Nigeria, Maldives, Azerbaijan) could not give equal rights to women in family life and continue to treat them as their subordinates. Many countries could not understand the spirit behind the concept of polygamy, and gave a free hand to men to marry four women at a time (Maldives, Arabia, Pakistan, Azerbaijan). In Islam the husband has the financial responsibility of the family but in many countries, it was interpreted very narrowly, depriving women of the opportunity to contribute to the national economy. Islam gave importance to Motherhood, but it does not mean to put women in the four walls of the house, as many Muslim think. My study revealed that most of the Muslim States, have not correctly understood the Islamic philosophy behind the concept of women's role in the family and the world at large. The world is changing and progressing very fast, and so also its requirements. The rights and duties of women have to be re-defined and re-adjusted to the changing needs of the world, within the prescribed boundaries of Islam. In practically all the countries right from the beginning there have been great variations in the rights of the Muslim women at different stages. The changes depend on the whims and fancies of the ruling parties. Never in the past, has any sincere attempt been made to bring Islamic scholars together to look into the spirit of the Quranic messages. Most of the interpretations of the Quran were given by male members only and women were not given the chance to represent their view point. Right from the beginning this world is under the male domination (mostly because of their physical strength) and it is

The Status of Women In The Muslim World

not easy to come out of their clutches, and disturb the balance of power. But now it is high time that the world should realize that men and women are equal before God. He does not discriminate on the basis of sex; hence this principle should be extended in all the phasis of life. The functions and the role of husband and wife should be clearly demarcated, with each one having his/her free zone to work. The role need not to be identical but based on the strength and weaknesses of each other. Further, the role should not be competitive but should be complementary to each other. I strongly, recommend and request specially Organization of Islamic Cooperation (OIC) to form a committee of Muslim scholars (both men and women) to reinterpret and re-design the functions and responsibilities of husband and wives in the light of the Quran and Sunnah. The world is eagerly looking forward to a working plan to provide peace and prosperity to the world, but the strength has to be provided from the foundation - the family. A happy and prosperous family will provide peace and prosperity not only to its members but to the community as a whole.

Women's Participation in Politics: -

Politics has always been considered as men' job, even today, in ten EU Member States - Bulgaria, Czech Republic, Estonia, Cyprus, Ireland, Latvia, Hungary, Malta, Romania and Slovakia - men make up at least 80% of the national parliament[4]. Irish and England were the first to grant the right to vote to women (1818) followed by New Zealand (1893) and Australia (1894). Azerbaijan (1915) was the first Muslim majority country to grant universal suffrage[5]. After IInd world war one by one all the countries started giving the right to vote to women. Saudi Arabia was the last one to grant (2015.)
(The Right to Vote in the world. Appendix V)

After the IInd world war with the establishment of U.N and its allied agencies great pressure was put on the countries, for the political participation of women. The Convention on the Elimination of All Forms of Discrimination Against Women

(CEDAW) emphasized women's rights to participate in political decision-making.

"Shall ensure to women on equal terms with men, the right to participate in the formation of government policy and the implementation thereof and to hold public office and perform all public functions at all levels of government..."

The Beijing Declaration and Platform for Action of 1995, which is the most visionary agenda for the empowerment of women and was adopted by 189 countries, strongly emphasized the need for women's participation in the decision-making process. Then there was a wave of uprising among Muslim countries which pave the way for easing involvement of women in parliament. There has been a gradual increase in the number of women in parliament. Many Muslim countries adopted the quota system to ensure the presence of women in parliament. The countries which have a high percentage of women in parliament (see Appendix11) are Rwanda (61.3 % which is not a Muslim country but it has a large number of Muslim population) Cuba (53.2 %) Bolivia (53.1 %)[6].

The Beijing Declaration has set the base platform for Action 1995 of 30% seats for women in parliament. Many Muslim countries like Tunisia (317) Sudan (309) Uganda (34.9) have met the baseline. In 2013 for the first time 30 women were appointed to Saudi Arabia's Shure Council bringing the percentage to 20%, whereas the record of some Muslim countries like Kuwait (3%) Oman and Yemen (1% each) is very low[7].

One important question is do these women in parliament represent the views of the women and are able to safeguard their interests or they have to confirm themselves to their party agenda irrespective of women's interest. Appendix 111 shows that there were at least a dozen women who were either Prime Minister or President at some point of time in Muslim countries. The important question is what was the contribution of these women towards the rights and status of women.

Indonesia, Turkey, Bangladesh, Iran and Mauritius all had women as head of the state at some point of time, but they represented the citizens in general not the women in particular.

Benazir Bhutto was twice the Prime Minister of Pakistan (1988-90 & 1993-96) Begum Khalida Zia (1991-2000) of Bangladesh served more than one term as Prime Minister. In all these cases they had the support of powerful political dynasties and came into power after their father or husbands had been killed. They continue to pursue the policies of their parties, which did not prioritize women's rights. It shows that it does not matter who is in power but the importance is of the policies and agenda of the particular party in power.
(Muslim Women Political leaders Appendix V1)

Crown Prince Mohammad bin Salman of Saudi Arabia has extended many rights to Saudi women bringing the Saudi Arabia on par with other Muslim countries. Is this step because of his conviction on the role of women or the intention of playing a significant role in international politics, whatever may be the reason, there is no denial of the fact that it has made a deep impact on the status of women in Muslim world. The Physical presence of women in parliament does bring a moral pressure on government and the public to safeguard and enhance women's rights, hence Muslim countries should encourage women's participation in politics and try to reach at least the target of 30 % laid down by the U N.

The Need for Reforms in Family laws: -

In Muslim countries Family laws are generally governed by Shariah. As mentioned earlier Shariah laws are not codified and differ from country to country and from time to time. The Family laws, generally include subjects like, marriage, polygamy, divorce child custody and inheritance. Some countries have introduced reforms in it, but even then, there are many loopholes in the system and need drastic changes.

In Islam women have the right to choose their life partner. In some countries the consent of the girl is necessary, in some other, father or guardian's consent is also essential. Here comes the clash, and many a time the girl loses her right to choose her partner and results in forced marriage, which is against the Quranic concept.

Child Marriage: -

Child Marriage is of great concern not only for Muslim countries but for the whole world. Child marriage is allowed in more than 100 countries including the United States, according to the United Nations Populations Fund (UNFPA) and the U.N International Children's Emergency Fund) over 700 million women currently living got married while they were just children.

Child marriage hurts young women's health, education and long-term ability to earn an income and is considered a human rights' violation. Yet law in over 116 countries allows people under the age of 18 to wed[8].

In Islam there is no minimum age for marriage, it depends on the physical maturity of the girls which differ from region to region. In Arabian countries it was a tradition to get girls married at an earlier age.

In many Muslim countries the minimum age of marriage now has been fixed at 16 or 18 years but the traditions and the custom over rule this. According to UNICEF (2018) Report, Africa has the highest incident rate of child marriage (under 18yrs) which is over 70%[9]. Bangladesh also has a very high number of child marriage[10]. In Azerbaijan, Maldives, Iran, Pakistan, Nigeria Saudi Arabia, Afghanistan, Indonesia - child marriage is a common phenomenon. In Morocco while in personal law quite a few significant changes have been introduced but tradition takes over the law and over 41000 child marriage take place every year[11].

In Malaysia a 41-year-old Malaysian wedded an 11-year-old girl, the man already had two wives and six children. Over half of Yemeni girls get married before 18, some by the age of eight[12].

It is high time that Muslim countries take this issue of child marriage seriously and make every effort to stop this undesirable practice. The government should realize that law alone will not be an effective step. There is a need to create an awareness among the people of the serious consequences of early marriage. It deprives the girl of her right to education. It is a violation of her fundamental right, and above all the adverse consequences of health on her personality and her future prospects in life.

In many Muslim countries by laws are not laid down properly giving a free hand to law enforcing agency to use their discretion in favor of male members. It is necessary not only to bring changes in the law books but also to see that these laws are implemented in the right spirit which requires an enlightened orientation program for employees at all the levels. The focus should be to change the mind setup.

The laws on polygamy differ from country to country, Tunisia and Turkey have abolished polygamy in the law books. In many other countries also such as Kyrgyzstan, Tajikistan, and Uzbekistan, it is prohibited by law but still there are backdoor methods. In some countries like Algeria, Bangladesh, Pakistan, Iraq, Jordan, Morocco, and Singapore, court's permission for a second marriage is necessary. In Iran spousal consent for a second marriage is required. In Saudi Arabia, and Nigeria no permission is necessary. In Saudi Arabia at least half a million men have second wife It is noted that even though there are restrictions for second marriage it is not difficult to overcome them, for example to take spouse's consent or to get the court's permission for the second marriage. It is pointed out that in many cases the first wife does not get proper maintenance and there is no way to ascertain it.

Right to Divorce: -

In most of the states it is the unilateral right of men to divorce women. The most common method is to orally pronounce, without even assigning the reasons (e.g. Brunei Darussalam, Iran). In some countries law require that they should register after giving divorce (Azerbaijan, Brunei Darussalam) in some others before the pronouncement. But in practically all the countries the women's right to divorce is very limited. In some countries even for registration of application for divorce the consent of husband is essential (Azerbaijan) if he does not give permission the application cannot be registered. In all the cases the only option left to women is to apply for Khula without any financial implications. In some states (Azerbaijan) even for Khula husband's permission is essential, if he doesn't give permission the wife has to live like a prisoner all her life.

In some states, the law clearly discriminates and deprives the women of her rights e.g. in Brunei Darussalam it is very easy for husbands to give divorce outside the court, he is only required to register it within a week. The wife can apply for divorce in a court but its registration depends on the consent of the husband, if he does not give consent, the court cannot register it, the only alternative for the wife is to apply for Khula,

In Tunisia and Turkey, both the spouses have the right to file for divorce through court. Divorce through unilateral reputation (Talaq) by husband is not recognized. The Muslim countries should take the matter seriously and see that women also get the same right to divorce as men.

Education for Girls/ Women: -

Girl's education is pivotal for the development of society. It is a strategic development priority, U.N organizations aim to enforce basic human rights including education for all. The International Bill of Human Rights contains provisions on compulsory and free primary education and on non-discrimination in education (U.N General Assembly, 1948). The Convention on the Elimination of all Forms of Discrimination Against Women (U.N. General Assembly 1979) and Convention on the Rights of the Child (1989) contain the most comprehensive set of legally enforceable commitments, concerning both the rights to education and to gender equality. The Jomtien Declaration (UNESCO 1990), Dakar Framework for Action (UNESCO 2000B) and Millennium Development Goals (2000), all have emphasized early childhood care and education.

Practically all Muslim countries are party to these international commitments. Many of the Muslim countries like Azerbaijan, Morocco, Tunisia have committed themselves for the free and compulsory education for boys and girls. Some of the Muslim states are doing very well in the field of girl's education and one of them is Bangladesh[13]. There are many other

Muslim countries like Indonesia, Kuwait, UAE, Azerbaijan, Bahrain, Brunei and Libya which have a good record of girl's education. In Morocco primary education of girls has gone up to 112% (2012) from 52% (1991).

As per Global Gender Gap Index there are also many Muslim countries which are lagging behind in this sphere, like Saudi Arabia (127) Iran (130) Pakistan (135).

There are some countries like Nigeria, Pakistan, Ethiopia, Cole D Ivoire, Burkina, Faso, Niger and Yemen which are worst for child school attendance rate[14]. According to UNESCO 130 million girls between the age of 6 and 17are out of school and 15 million girls of primary school age - half of them in sub-Saharan Africa - will never enter school[15].

In the sphere of education, a great variation is found in the urban and rural regions of many countries. E.g. in Nigeria, only 4% of young women in the North West Zone can read compared to 99% of women in the South East[16].

In Morocco primary education for Girls has gone up to 112% (2012) but in rural areas 90% of girls are illiterate. In many countries like Afghanistan, Pakistan, Iran and Nigeria, the problems in the field of primary and secondary education are more or less the same. In many places' poverty is the main cause, especially when the choice comes between the education of son and daughter. In many places there is scarcity of girl's schools, the distance of schools, the problem of transportation and above all the question of safety of girls, are the main hurdles. In Afghanistan, Pakistan and Nigeria there is always a threat to the life of the girl students. Of late in some countries, steps have been taken to solve some of these problems by opening new schools for girls[17].

In the sphere of higher education for girls in the last two decades there has been appreciable progress in many Muslim countries. In Saudi Arabia which was supposed to be lacking in the field of women's rights and where only 2% of young women went to the University in 1970, today the figure has fumed to 57% that is on par with the U.S takers in 1983 and more than Mexico, China, Brazil or India[18]. In Brunei Darussalam girls have surpassed boys in university education. In Algeria, the percentage of women among university graduates has risen from 20% to 40%. Something similar has happened in Iran, of course Pakistan and Saharan Africa are trailing behind in this field[19].

The type of education which these young university women are choosing is also of considerable significance. There are only five universities in the world, where women have surpassed men in the field of science, technology and engineering, and two of them- Kuwait and Brunel, are predominantly Muslim[20].

It is noted that in many Muslim countries like Afghanistan, Pakistan and Morocco there are great variations in the girl's education from region to region and among different levels of education. In some countries like Saudi Arabia, Iran and Turkey great importance is attached to higher education but there is no comprehensive planning and no correlation between education and employment, and between demand and supply, with the result that a large number of university graduates face unemployment.

The educational policy of a country for girls should be based on long-term planning, taking into account the role, women are expected to play.

Some Muslim countries like Saudi Arab, Iran and Turkey in their zeal to focus attention on women's education have adopted a very liberal scholarship policy where a large number of women are granted scholarships to pursue higher education in countries like United States, England and Australia. But on their return these women do not find a bright future in their countries, as generally there is no correlation between the degrees, they have obtained in foreign countries and the job opportunities in their own country. This leads to frustration, which needs to be rectified.

The Need to Incorporate Quranic knowledge in School's Syllabus: -

All Muslims believe in the Quran. Most of them read the Quran in Arabic language, and pray Salah without understanding its meaning, as they do not know Arabic language. The crux of the problem is that they do not understand the message of God and are not able to practice it in the day-to-day life. This is the main reason for not being a practicing Muslim. I strongly suggest that in Muslim countries in all schools, a detailed knowledge of the Quran and Sunnah in the regional languages must be a compulsory subject. This will enable the children to have a correct understanding of the Quranic message. Besides this, in high school, there should be a separate subject on some specific issues, like rights and duties of husband and wife, role of family etc. to make the young generation prepare for future life.

What is happening today, is that with half knowledge, they pick up a subject, and implement it wrongly e.g. most of the people believe that the Quran has given a free hand for polygamy, without realizing the conditions laid down for it, which is a wrong assumption.

What is needed is the correct knowledge and perspective so that the young generation can build a strong and happy foundation of the family life, which is an essential step for the prosperity and happiness of the world at large.

Women's Role in the Executive Branch of Government: -

There was a gradual increase in employment of women in executive branch in Muslim countries, though mostly they were given jobs in soft portfolios like education and health. In Maurita in 2017 women have the largest share of 26 ministries, in the United Arab Emirate women enjoy a share of 27%, in Tunisia 23% of women are involved in the executive branch. There is no cabinet Minister in Saudi Arab and Camaros[21]. Women are inducted into the public service of all the countries. Morocco has a large civil service and the percentage of women is 39%. In Tunisia (2014) also 37% of women are involved in bureaucracy followed by Egypt (36%), and Azerbaijan (2017) 28.7%.

In civil service the concentration of women is more at the lower level. It is noted that the number of women decreases as they climb the ladder. but this is not confined to Muslim countries it is global trend in USA and Europe also.

In many countries women's share in foreign affairs is increasing for example in UAE there were three women ambassadors in 2016. At present Saudi Arabia has 2 women ambassadors one in United Sates and another in Norway. Another significant feature is women's share in judiciary In Algeria in 2016 one third seats were occupied by women, in Morocco also 20% women are in judiciary. In Bahrain and Egypt also of late women have been appointed in Judiciary[22].

A strong bureaucracy is the backbone of the country. Legislature lays down the laws but they are administered by the bureaucracy and much depends on the attitude of law enforcement agencies. History is full of examples when the negative attitude of bureaucracy has defeated the very purpose of a law. Today there are a number of examples which can be cited in this regard such as child marriage, honor killing, rape and domestic violence, the way the laws are implemented by the bureaucracy using its discretion has upset the whole program. The reports of the international organizations like United Nations Population Fund (UNFPA) and UNESCO and others have repeatedly pointed out this lapse.

In most of the Muslim countries, the law enforcement agencies - the police and the courts-have a very negative attitude specially towards the victims of rape and domestic violence. Many a time they even refuse to register a FIR, and generally no proper investigation is done. The victims are treated as accused, with the result women do not like to report a case and prefer to suffer in silence.

Many of these problems can be solved if there is a strong motivated bureaucracy-consisting of women who can take a positive attitude towards these problems. As seen above in most of the Muslim countries the number of women in civil services specially at the decision-making level is very low. An attempt should be made to increase the number at all levels of bureaucracy to save guard the interests of women, which in most of the cases is being damaged by the male dominated bureaucracy.

Female Labor Force Participation: -

There is great variation in female labor force participation in Muslim majority countries. There are countries like Bangladesh (57%) Indonesia (51%) and Nigeria (48%) where the women's share is nearly 50% or above, while in many others like Syria (13%), Iraq (14%), Iran (16%), Afghanistan (16%) and Saudi Arabia (17%)[25], it is much below the international level (34.9 %).

According to the World Economic Forum (2012) Report, Islamic nations in the Middle East and North Africa region are trying to increase economic employment opportunities for women but compared to other regions of the world, the MENA region ranks lowest in economic participation, employment and political empowerment of women[26]. Ten countries with the lowest women labor force participation in the world - Jordan, Oman, Morocco, Iran, Turkey, Algeria, Yemen, Saudi Arabia, Pakistan and Syria - are Islamic countries[27].

(Female Labor force in Muslim World. Appendix V11.)

In some cases where women have the right to work and are educated, women's job opportunities are unequal as compared to men. In Egypt, for example, women have limited opportunities to work in the private sector as women are expected to put their role in the family first[28].

The unemployment rate of female workers in Muslims majority countries is pretty high, Syria tops the list (24.2%) followed by Iraq (22.5%) in many other countries also the situation is not satisfactory.

(Female Unemployment rate in Muslim Countries. Appendix V111.)

The Muslim countries need to work out a comprehensive employment plan for women taking into account the economic and cultural needs of the country. The government should also focus attention on the dual role of women as mother and working wife and try to provide facilities such as long-term maternity leave, day care centers, transportation etc. to make their jobs easy.

Women Entrepreneurs: -

As noted above, in most of the Muslim majority states, the women's contribution in the formal economic sphere is very low. The world recognizes the critical role of women's economic empowerment in achieving prosperity and peace. Societies that empower women to participate fully in civic and economic life are more prosperous and peaceful. It is believed that investment in gender equality and women's empowerment can help eradicate extreme poverty, built economies unlock human potential in a transformation scale.

In Muslim states there are many reasons for the low involvement of women in economic field. Some states have rigid customs and traditions, some have strict rules and regulations like guardianship, some have restrictions on women's movements, and some others have the problem of segregation, where women are not preferred to work along with men. And at many places the importance of motherhood and the need to take care of children and home comes in the way of women's employment

In many countries there is a big difference in educational facilities for women in urban and rural areas, with the result there are very limited employment opportunities for them. Of late the Covid19 has badly hit the economy worldwide, there are millions of people without jobs. In these economic crisis's governments have to find some alternative avenues for women. Women's entrepreneurs are an emerging worldwide market force and job creation. It was found that the gender gap in business ownership remains high in many economies around the world. The gap in female entrepreneurship is especially apparent in low-income economies where women are much less likely than men to start a

new business The World Bank Database report pointed out that the biggest gap is in the Middle East and North African Region. It also highlighted that in the last five years there has been a steady rise in women entrepreneurs in countries like Morocco, Jordan, and the United Arab Emirates.
(The Muslim Female Entrepreneurs Appendix 1X.)

In Muslim countries in view of the big gender gap, legal disparities and traditional barriers, it is desirable that governments should concentrate on women's entrepreneurs and provide government policy, technical knowledge and legal advice.

The investment in women's entrepreneur will have a far-reaching effect not only on the nation's economy but will make women's position strong in the family. The economic gains will also be fruitful for education and health of the family. It may also help to reduce the child labor and drop off the girls from school.

Women as An Agent of Change: -

Women have to realize that from the beginning they are living in a patriarchal society where the decision-making power is with the male members. Men were using rather abusing women for the sake of their own benefits. They have given her the rights and benefits to a certain extent beyond which it is their dominion.

The international organizations have been trying hard for the last several years to bring Gender Equality but today not a single country in the world can claim that it has achieved Gender Equality. There are many countries which have a long list of laws protecting women's rights. Most of the countries are signatories to the International documents. These agreements repeatedly put emphasis on the question of gender equality and by signing these documents the countries are committed to create an atmosphere of equitable justice for women.

Most of the Muslim countries are signatories to these documents but when it comes to practice the things are different. Most of these laws are overruled by custom and traditions whether it is question of child marriage, honor killing, relationship within the family, choice of career and employment or domestic violence.

Women have to understand the reality that it is not easy to change their status. Men would not like to share their power of decision making with women but it has to come, at least in some areas as family matters and those which concern women's personality development and career. But this change cannot be brought by force - it is the will and not the force, which is the basis of law.

In order to bring this change, there is a need for creating awareness among all sections of society, the positive effects of education, health and economic participation of women. Advancement of women is the indication of the advancement of the nation. The success of it depends on the thinking and attitude of the people. This is a silent peaceful revolution to be brought with love, affection and patience.

Violence Against Women: -

The U.N Declaration on the Elimination of Violence Against Women states "Violence Against Women is a manifestation of historically unequal power relations between men and women" and "violence against women is one of the crucial social mechanism by which women are forced into sub ordinate position compared to men"[29].

Kofi Annan, Secretary General of the U.N declared in a (2006) report on the U.N Development Fund for Women (UNIFEM) website. "Violence against women and girls is a problem of pandemic proportions. At least one out of every three women around the world has been beaten, coerced into sex or otherwise abused in her lifetime with the abuser usually someone known to her[30]." The above statements clearly indicate that violence against women is a global problem, not confined to the Muslim world only.

In the most advanced countries of the world like the USA, in one year (2005) more than 181 women were killed by their intimate partners. In France, England and Wales more than 100 women are killed every year[32].

Hundreds of women are murdered by their families each year in the name of family "honor". Reports submitted to the U.N Commission on Human Rights show that honor killings have occurred in Bangladesh, Great Britain, Brazil, Ecuador, Egypt, India, Israel, Italy, Pakistan, Morocco, Sweden, Turkey and Uganda[33]. The Human Rights activists say honor killings and dowry deaths (India) are the part of problems of violence against women.

In Arabia and many other Muslim countries, domestic violence is not yet considered a major concern despite its increasing frequency and serious consequences. Surveys in Egypt, Palestine, Israel and Tunisia show that at least one out of three women is beaten by their husbands. This indifference to this type of violence stems from the attitude that domestic violence is a private matter and usually a justifiable response to misbehavior on the part of the wife. This is also supportive from the selective excerpts from the Quran, (4.34, beating the wife) which has not been properly interpreted.

These religions justifications plus the importance of preserving the honor of the family, tend abusers, police and other law enforcement personnel to join a conspiracy of silence rather than disclosing these offences. It is the responsibility of all, especially the Islamic scholars, to place a correct picture of the Islamic society. Islam has given equal rights to women in practically every sphere of life. Islam is for peace, there is no scope for domestic violence in a true Islamic family. The relationship between husband and wife has to be understood in its proper context. Domestic violence is the result of ignorance or half knowledge of the Quranic rules. An awareness of gender equality in the light of the Quran and Sunnah is a prerequisite for the development of human rights. unless the society as a whole is convinced of this state of affairs, gender equality cannot be achieved.

The Role of Women Police: -

The violence against women is a burning topic all over the world, despite great efforts made by International and national bodies, it is still an alarming subject. In most of the Muslim countries, it was found that the role of law enforcing agency is not satisfactory. Women do not want to lodge a complaint to the police because of its negative attitude. In many cases the complaint is not even registered, because police take it lightly as a family matter; even if it is registered, no action is taken against the culprit. Many a time for lack of evidence or some other reason, the victim is turned into a culprit and punished.

It was pointed out by many, that these police personnel neither have adequate knowledge of the laws against violence nor do they have the skill to deal with this subject. Apart from this the major problem is the attitude of the police personnel. All over the world, they are known for their brutality, roughness and inhuman treatment. They lack the attitude to understand the female problems in their proper context. Here we need someone who can understand the problem, give a patient hearing and have sympathy with the victim.

It is because of this perception women were inducted into police forces, all over the world. But it is noted that in most of the countries, the government does not make proper use of women's talent in this field. Many women after joining the police force lose their feminine qualities and become as tough and arrogant as male police officers, which defeats the very purpose of inducting the female into the police force.

Women in general and Muslim women in particular feel shy to discuss their personal problems with male members. In this regard I suggest that a separate cadre of women in policing on line with Indian experiment, may be established in all Muslim states, to deal only with cases of violence against women, this will encourage the women to report the cases and get the redressal done.

This will also have a far-reaching impact on family relations and will reduce the male domination. But care has to be taken to see that these women police do not give up their feminine qualities such as patience, sympathy, sensitivity and understanding of the family problems and become another man police.

The Role of Organization of Islamic Cooperation (O.I.C): -

The OIC was founded in 1916 with the membership of 53 Muslims majority countries. It is the collective voice of the Muslim world in the spirit of promoting international peace and harmony. The Organization of Islamic Cooperation has permanent delegates to U.N. It has its headquarters at Jeddah, and holds an Islamic summit once in three months. While the organization has been known for its cultural and social projects, its political influence has been relatively limited. It doesn't have a unified voice, policies of individual countries greatly differ[34].

Today it is a great challenge for Organization of Islamic Cooperation to focus its attention on the status of women in the Muslim world. Most of the members of O.I.C are also the members of the U.N. Commission on the status of women (1946) which is a functional commission of the ECOSOC. The CSW is the principal global intergovernmental body, exclusively dedicated to the empowerment of women. In April 2017, ECOSO elected 13 new members including Saudi Arabia, which was a target of attack by many, for its treatment of women.

While many members of Organization of Islamic Cooperation take part in the deliberations of the Commission on the Status of Women, and are signatories to its resolutions, but when it comes to implementation of resolutions, the progress is very slow. The OIC has not taken any lead in focusing the women's problems in the Muslim world.

The Muslim countries are spread in different regions of the world with great differences in their political, socio-economic and cultural practices. Islam is the religion of all Muslims even though many countries do not make a commitment in their constitutions. In most of the countries there is a dual system of law - the civil law and the Shariah law - but the interpretation of Shariah law differs from country to country bringing a difference in the personal laws of women. It is observed that in most of the countries, Quranic laws (pertaining to husband-wife relations, divorce or domestic violence) have not been interpreted in the right spirit of the Quranic message, hence, there is a need to interpret them in the light of the present socio-economic structure of the society and to codify them.

As per my knowledge there is no Muslim State which has depicted correctly the rights and the status of women as per the rules and regulations of the Quran and Sunnah. Women nowhere enjoy the equal status as laid down in the Quran. The concept of family has been diluted. The domestic violence, which has no basis in Islam, is the common feature of husband wife relationship.

Today women are victims of great hardship. They are being crushed under the wheels of modern society, trying to balance their roles as wife, mother and working woman. The family life has come at the crossroad, the children are without emotional and moral support from their parents. There is always tension, and a vacuum in the family and the society at large.

This is the time when the members of Organization of Islamic Cooperation should come forward and with the help of scholars (both men and women) provide a true picture of the distribution of functions and the positive role of men and women as provided by the Quran and Sunnah in the family and society at large.

The International organizations for the past so many decades have been trying hard to overcome these problems of social life, but they have not succeeded. There is chaos everywhere. No society is at peace. The peace and happiness in the society can be brought by women only. The women have to be an agent of change, but this needs a drastic change and the awareness among the men and the society as a whole of the proper role of men and women.

The Organization of Islamic Cooperation with a population of over 1.8 billion can be a strong pressure group and can save the world from the crisis which it is facing today, if it is able to work out a model of healthy and balanced relationship between the wife and husband. The Quran has answers for every problem. The need is to understand it and practice it in the right perspective.

A Request to Richest Royal Rulers of the Muslim World: -

It is so heartening to know that the ten richest Royals of the World are from the Muslim World. God has given them abundance of wealth due to the natural resources of oil and gas. Their personal assists run into billions (King of Thailand 30 billion, Sultan of Brunei Darussalam, 20 billion, King of Saudi Arabia, 18 billion). See Appendix 10 for more information

The citizens of these countries are happy that they enjoy many amenities, like free education, public health, housing, etc. which are not available to the citizens of many other countries. But when I see the lifestyle of these rulers - the most expensive palaces, the number of luxury cars, which runs into thousands, extensive use of gold in their aircraft, cars and household goods including toilets - I feel embarrassed. They are no doubt entitled to live a comfortable lifestyle but is this lifestyle in accordance with the principles of the Quran and Sunnah. They are the leaders of the Muslim Community what message do they wish to pass on to their people. My humble request to these Royal rulers is to, please cut down your expenses just by 20% and donate the money for the welfare of Muslim community. I am hopeful in the period of next 10 years there will not be any illiterate or hungry person in Muslim community. Since all these states are the members of Organization of Islamic Cooperation, I request that organization to take a lead in this direction and establish a fund. Muslim history will always remember this act of kindness and they will be rewarded by God in their eternal life.

Shamim Aleem

The Need for Orientation and Awareness Programs: -

Our efforts to bring a change in the structure of the status of women, in accordance with the broad principles of the Quran and Sunnah and to see that this model works in the present-day society is a big challenge. The first requirement is that there should be a clear-cut idea of our goals and limitations. The plan of action has to be accepted by men and women, both. Adding a new plan in the law books will not solve the problem. There should be a change in the thinking and attitude of people at every level. But this is the most difficult task. It needs a lot of homework and effort.

As suggested earlier, the first dose of medicine should begin from school, the young generation should be very clear about the structure of Muslim society and their own role in it. Secondly all those persons who are involved in the implementation of policies and programs - law enforcement agencies, judiciary - should not only have a clear idea about these plans but should be convinced of its importance. And the community at large should also be convinced of its significance.

In this process not only government agencies but NGOs also have an important role to play. The people have to be reached through different methods-newspaper, radio, T.V., Internet documentaries and local entertainment platforms. The different agencies should project the same program. Once people are convinced, success will not be difficult. But to convince the people, and to make them accept the new challenges is no doubt difficult but not impossible, if one has the determination to do it.

3

Appendix

I. Muslim Majority Countries

INDONESIA, PAKISTAN, BANGLADESH, NIGERIA, EGYPT, Iran, Turkey, Algeria, Sudan, Saudi Arabia, Yemen, Uzbekistan, Niger, Mali, Syria, Malaysia, Senegal, Kazakhstan, Burkina Faso, Tunisia, Somalia, Guinea, Jordan, Azerbaijan, Chad, Tajikistan, Libya, Sierra Leone, Turkmenistan, Kyrgyzstan, United Arab Emirates, Mauritania, Lebanon, Oman, Kuwait, Albania, Qatar, Bahrain, Djibouti, Western Sahara, Maldives, Brunei, Mayotte

II. Influential Women in Islamic History

1.Khadija Bint e Khuwaylid (d. 620)

Even before her marriage to the Prophet Mohammad (S) she was an important figure in her own right, being a successful merchant and one of the elite figures in Mecca. She played a central role in supporting and propagating the new faith of Islam and has the distinction of being the first Muslim.

2. Nusaybah Bint e Ka'ba Al-Ansariyya (d.634)

Also known as Umm Ammara, she was a member of the Banu Najjar tribe. She took part in the Battle of Uhud (625) in which she carried a sword and shield and fought against the Meccans. She shielded the Prophet from enemies and even sustained several lance wounds and arrows as she cast herself in front of him to protect him.

3. KhawlaBint e Al Azwar (d. 639)

Another contemporary of the Prophet. She participated in the Battle of Yarmouk (636) against the Byzantines.

4. Aisha Bint e Abu-Bakr (d.678)

She was the wife of prophet Mohammad(S) and needs no introduction. She served the Muslim community after the death of Prophet for _____ years. She was the most scholarly woman.

5. Zaynab Bint e Ali (d. 681)

She was the grand-daughter of the Prophet and daughter of his daughter Fatima. She played a central role both during and after the Massacre at Karbala (680). Her strength, patience and wisdom make her one of the most important women in early Islam.

6. Rabia Al Adawiyya (d. 801)

One of the most important mystics in the Muslim traditions. She is considered to be one of the founders of the Sufi School of 'Divine Love".

7. Lubna of Cordoba (d. 984)

Originally a slave-girl of Spanish origin, she was one of the most important figures in the Umayyad palace in Cordoba. She was a skilled mathematician. She excelled in writing, grammar and poetry.

8. Al-Malika Al -Hurrah Arwa Al-Salehi (d.1138)

She ruled as the queen of Yemen from 1067 to 1138. She was well-versed in various religious sciences, the Quran, hadith, poetry and history.

9. Fatima Bint e Abid-Qassim Abdul Al-Rehman Bint e Mohammad Bint e Ghalib Al-AnsarialSharrat (d. 1216)

She was one of the most learned women in Al-Andalus during the late twelfth and early thirteenth centuries. She was well versed with legal theory, jurisprudence and mysticism.

10. Razia Sultan (d. 1240)

She was the ruler of the Sultanate of Delhi between 1236 and 1240. Her father shams Al-Din Iltutmish designated her the official ruler, before his death. She was a fairly effective ruler and a major patron of learning establishing schools and libraries across north India. She was overthrown in a rebellion by the nobles of the Kingdom and killed.

11. Shajar Al-Durr (d. 1257)

She was the widow of the Ayyubid Sultan Al-Salih Ayyub (R. 1240-1249) and played an important role in Egyptian politics following her husband's death.

12. Zainab Bint e Ahmad (d.1339)

She was perhaps one of the most eminent Islamic scholars of the fourteenth century. She belonged to the Hanbali school of jurisprudence and resided in Damascus.

13. Sayyida Al-Hurrah (d.1542)

She was originally from the Nasrid Kingdom of Granada but was forced to flee following its conquest by Christian, Spain in 1492. She settled in Morocco and along with her husband fortified and ruled the town of Tetouan on the north coast. Following the death of her husband in 1515, she became the sole ruler of the city.

14. Pari Khan Khanum (d. 1578)

A Safavid princess and daughter of Shah Tahmasp, she was the most influential Iranian woman in the sixteenth century.

15. Kosem Sultan (d. 1651)

She was the consort (then wife) of Ottoman Sultan Ahmed I, the mother of the Sultan's Murad IV. She was the most powerful woman in Ottoman history. Between 1623 and 1632. She served as regent for her son Murad IV. She was assassinated in 1651. [Source; 15 important Muslim Women in History, Ballandalus, 2014.]

III. Countries with the Most Maternity Leave

Countries with Most Maternity leave – March 2019		
Sweden	480 days	80% up to 390 days
Norway	400 days	80 – 100 %
Croatia	365 days	100 %
U. K	365 days	90% first of 6 weeks
Serbia	365 days	100 %

IV. Countries with the Least Maternity Leave

Countries with Least Maternity Leave	
U.A. E	6 weeks
Switzerland	12 weeks
U.S. A	12 weeks
Germany	14 weeks
Belgium	15 weeks

V. Right to Vote to Women in Muslim World

Muslim Countries	Year	
Saudi Arabia	2015	
Syria	1949	Some women
Egypt	1956	All women

Tunisia	1959	
Mauritania	1961	
Iran	1963	
Azerbaijan	1918	First Muslim Country
Pakistan	1947	
South Africa	1944	
Kuwait	2005	
United Arab Emirates	2006	

VI. Muslim Women - Head of Government/State

Head of Govt./State	Country	Status	In Office (1st Time)
Benazir Bhutto	Pakistan	Prime Minster	2nd December 1988 – 6th August 1990
Khaleda Zia	Bangladesh	Prime Minister	20th March 1991 – 30th March 1996
Tansu Ciller	Turkey	Prime Minister	25th June 1993- 6th March 1996
Sheikh Hasina	Bangladesh	Prime Minister	23 June 1996 -15 July 2001
MameMadiorBoye	Senegal	Prime Minister	03 March 2001- 04 November 2002
Megawati Soekarnoputri	Indonesia	President	23 July 2001 - 20 October 2004
Roza Otunbayeva	Kyrgyzstan	President	23 July 2001 - 20 October 2004
AtifeteJahjaga	Kosovo	President	07 April 2011 - 07 April 2016
CisseMAriamKaidama Sidibe	Mali	Prime Minister	03 April 2011 - 22 March 2012

Sibel Siber	Northern Cyprus	Prime Minister	13 June 2013 - 02 September 2013
Aminata Toure	Senegal	Prime Minister	03 September 2013 - 08 July 2014
Sheikh Hasina	Bangladesh	Prime Minister	06 January 2009 – incumbent
Ameenah Gurib	Mauritius	President	05 June 2015 - 23 March 2018
HalimahYacob	Singapore	President	14 September 2017 – incumbent
Source: Wikipedia, the free encyclopedia			

VII. Female Labor Force in Muslim World

Country	2008	2009	2010
Afghanistan	15%	15%	15%
Egypt	23%	24%	24%
Syria	14%	13%	13%
Iran	15%	15%	16%
Iraq	14%	14%	14%
Turkey	25%	27%	28%
Indonesia	51%	51%	51%
Tunisia	25%	25%	25%
Pakistan	22%	22%	22%
Bangladesh	56%	57%	57%
Saudi Arabia	17%	17%	17%
Nigeria	48%	48%	48%
Source: Global Gender Gap Report 2012, World Economic Forum			

VIII. Female Unemployment Rate in Muslim Countries

Country	2008	2009
Afghanistan	9.5% (2005)	---
Egypt	19.2%	22.9%
Syria	24.2%	2.3%
Iran	16.8%	--
Iraq	22.5% (2006)	--
Turkey	14.3%	13%
Indonesia	9.7%	8.5%
Tunisia	17.5% (2005)	--
Pakistan	8.6%	--
Bangladesh	7.4%	--
Saudi Arabia	13%	15.9%
Nigeria	--	--
Source: World Bank		

IX. Muslim Women Entrepreneurs

1.Sabah Nazi: -

Founder of Islamic Moments.

Credit: Muslim Lifestyle Expo. started her company in 2004. It has a wide range of greeting cards concentrated on Islamic Culture holidays and imagery.

2. Shahin Hussain: -

Started Mocktail company which produces non-alcoholic drinks.

3. Sheeza Shah: -

Founder of the UP Effect. It is involved with renewable energy, ethical fashion, and clear drinking water.

4. Muna Abu Sulaiman: -

She is host of Kalam Nawaem, one of the most popular shows in the Middle East. A Goodwill Ambassador of the U.N.

5. Asma Mansoor: -

Co-Founder of the Tunisian center for social Entrepreneurship, offers fellowship to those with new ideas.

6. Dana Al Taji: -

A Palestinian designer started to wear the Abaya (A full length cloak). She opened a boutique in Cairo.

7. Dr. Yasmeen Altaire: -

She is one of Saudi Arabia's most senior scientists and pioneers in the study of obesity, diabetes and mental health issues.

8. Esra Al Shafei: -

She is a leading internet activist in the Middle East. Based in Bahrain she is the founder of Migrant Rights.

9. Mali Alasousi: -

Kuwaiti based started her own tourism company. A triple Yemen in 2007 changed her life. She was so much affected by the poverty in Yemen that she sold her company and moved to Yemen and started an NGO to work on a range of social projects.

10. Yasmine El-Mehairy: -

She is Egyptian, created the Pan-Arab parenting site Super Mamma which offers an array for information ranging from pregnancy tips to cooking videos. Everything is written in Arabic.

11. Heidi Belal: -

She is from Egypt C-founded the web development from Code-Corner and then started the baked goods cookies.

X. 10 Richest Royals in the World

1. Bhumibol Adulyadej, King of Thailand - $ 43 billion (2014) (2020)
2. Hassanal Bolkiah, Sultan of Brunei - $ 20 billion
3. Abdullah Bin Abdul-Aziz Al Saud, Former King of Saudi Arabia - $ 18 billion
4. Khalifa Bin Zayed Al Nahyan, Amir of Abu Dhabi - $ 18 billion
5. Mohammad Bin Rashida Maktoum, Emir Sheikh of Dubai - $ 14 billion
6. Hasan Adam II, Prince of Liechtenstein - $ 4 billion
7. Hamad Bin Khalifa Al Thani, former Emir of Qatar - $ 2.4 billion
8. Albert II, Prince of Monaco - $ 1 billion
9. Shah Karim Al-Hussain Aga Khan IV of France - $ 800 millions
10. Qaboos Bin Said, Sultan of Oman - $ 700 million

Source: Times/Business June 2015
Top 10 Richest Royals in the World (2020) by Vrutika

\multicolumn{4}{c}{***Books Published by Prof. Shamim Aleem in English***}
S.no	Title	Year of Publication	Publisher
1.	Osmania University at Glance	2017	The Siasat Daily Hyderabad
2.	Women Peace and Security (An International Perspective)	2013	Xlibris-USA
3.	Prophet Muhammad(S) and his Family – A Sociological Perspective	2011	Authorhouse-USA
4.	Prophet Muhammad(S) and his Family – A Sociological Perspective	2008	IBS, New Delhi
5.	Women's Development Problems and Prospective	1996	APH Publishing Corporation, New Delhi
6.	The Suicide Problems & Remedies	1994	Ashish Publishing House, New Delhi
7.	Women Police and Social Changes	1991	Ashish Publishing House, New Delhi
8.	Women in Indian Police	19991	Gitanjali Publishing House, New Delhi
9.	State Administration in Andhra Pradesh	1988	Allied Published Pvt. Limited
10.	Developments in Administration under HEH. The Nizam VII.	1984	Osmania University, Press Hyderabad
11.	Personnel Management in a Princely State	1985	Gitanjali Publishing House, New Delhi

Books published by Prof. Shamim Aleem in Urdu			
S.no	Title	Year of Publication	Publisher
1.	Zindagi Kabhi Rukti Nahi	2016	Modern Publishing House, New Delhi
2.	Jag Aurat Jag	2013	Modern Publishing House, New Delhi
3.	Bikhray Moti	2013	Modern Publishing House, New Delhi
4.	Shamim Aleem Say Mileyay	2010	Modern Publishing House, New Delhi
5.	Mera Paygham Mohabbat Hai	2009	Modern Publishing House, New Delhi
6.	Sitaroon Se Agay	2007	Modern Publishing House, New Delhi
7.	Sondhi Mitti Ka Itir	2005	Modern Publishing House, New Delhi
8.	Aksay Kayenat	2002	Silver Line Printers, Hyderabad

Books Published by Prof. Shamim Aleem In Hindi			
S.no	Title	Year of Publication	Publisher
1.	Jag Aurat Jag	2013	Modern Publishing House, New Delhi

Printed in the United States
By Bookmasters